Bring Them Close

Selected Sermons by
Rabbi Elliot J. Cosgrove

Bring Them Close

Selected Sermons by
Rabbi Elliot J. Cosgrove

2019-2020/5780

PARK AVENUE SYNAGOGUE

Bring Them Close: Selected Sermons by Rabbi Elliot J. Cosgrove
2019-2020/5780

PARK AVENUE SYNAGOGUE

Copyright 2020 Park Avenue Synagogue
All rights reserved. No part of this publication may be reproduced, stored in a retrieval system, or transmitted in any form or by any means, electronic, mechanical, photocopying, recording or otherwise, without prior permission.

ISBN 978-0-9897672-8-6

Printed in the United States of America in 2020

Park Avenue Synagogue
50 East 87th Street
New York, NY 10128
www.pasyn.org

Contents

Introduction	ix
Preface	xi
Shof'tim 5779 　　Something to Say	1
Nitzavim 5779 　　Say It Ain't So, Joe	7
Erev Rosh Hashanah 5780 　　Angels in Hardhats	13
Rosh Hashanah 　　If Not Now, Then When?	19
Yom Kippur 　　Do a Mitzvah!	29
Yom Kippur Yizkor 　　The Parochet	41
Sukkot, Day 1 　　Builders	46
Hol Ha-moed Sukkot 　　Jonah's Sukkah	52

B'reishit
  #OneYearLater   57

Noaḥ
  The Anxiety of Influence   63

Va-yera
  Bystanders and Upstanders   69

Va-yiggash
  Time to Step Up and March   75

B'shallaḥ
  Making Sense of Our Moment   82

Yitro
  Standing at Sinai   88

T'rumah
  Let There Be Disruption   94

T'tzavveh, Shabbat Zakhor
  Purim in the Time of Coronavirus   101

Va-yikra
  The Next Right Thing   107

Pesaḥ, 2nd Day
  The Question of Suffering   112

Shabbat Hol Ha-moed Pesaḥ
  Social Solidarity . . . Not Distancing   117

Sh'mini
  On Leadership   123

Tazri·a/M'tzora
    The Life and Legacy of Waldemar M.W. Haffkine   130

Aḥarei Mot/K'doshim
    Like I Told You, It's an Honor   137

Emor
    Dreams Deferred   143

B'har/B'ḥukkotai
    From Chancellor to Chancellor   150

Shavuot, Yizkor
    Together . . . Apart   158

Naso
    That's My Bible   163

Sh'laḥ L'kha
    Speaking Privately   169

Pinḥas
    First Base on Race   176

Our Hanukkah: Rededication of the 87th Street Building   182

Park Avenue Synagogue 138th Annual Meeting   186

Louis Jacobs: A Man for Our Time   192

Park Avenue Synagogue   196

Park Avenue Synagogue Board of Trustees,
Clergy & Staff, 2020–2021   198

Introduction

It is my privilege and great pleasure to introduce our annual volume of Rabbi Elliot Cosgrove's sermons, the twelfth since he became our rabbi at Park Avenue Synagogue.

The past year has been a one of upheaval for the entire world, for New York City, for the American Jewish community, and yes, for Park Avenue Synagogue, too. I have described the past twelve months as a roller coaster for our congregation. We moved back into our revitalized 87th Street building in time for the High Holidays. In December, we rededicated the building with great celebration only to move out in March owing to the coronavirus pandemic. Within days, we made the transition to a virtual campus where we have offered online worship, adult learning, and keynote events. As this volume goes to print, we are considering how we can best re-open our physical campus while maintaining our enhanced digital campus.

This past year, we also experienced a rise of antisemitism throughout the country and are living through a long overdue call to action on systemic racism. Throughout all these ups and downs, Rabbi Cosgrove has compelled us to think about what our Jewish values demand in response to the challenges of the time and to take action against injustice. In his sermons, one Shabbat after another, he calls on the lessons of the Torah and relates them to current and historical events, creating a spiritual guidepost for our Tikkun Olam efforts as we try as a congregation and as individuals to do our part to repair the world.

At the same time as the rabbi has directed our attention outward, he has promoted our congregational mission: to inspire, educate, and support our members toward living passion-filled Jewish lives. Teaching us about prayer, learning, observance, and acts of kindness, he encourages us to strengthen our friendships with fellow members, become involved with the New York Jewish community, recognize our bonds to all of American Jewry, maintain meaningful relationships with Israel and with Jewish communities throughout the world, and understand our connections to Jews throughout time.

I encourage you to develop your own thinking about the critical issues of today by considering Rabbi Cosgrove's analyses and by taking his recommendations to heart. In addition to reading the sermons in this book, you may also wish to listen to them on Park Avenue Podcast or watch and listen on the PAS website. I also hope you will join us on Shabbat, whether along with the thousands via livestream, or in person when we are able to experience the beautiful music and prayer of our services, hear Rabbi Cosgrove's sermons live, and engage in the Park Avenue Synagogue conversation.

Todah rabbah, Rabbi Cosgrove, for both challenging and comforting us with your thoughtful words.

B'shalom,

Marc Becker
Chairman of the Board

Preface

Just a few months before his tragic death, my dear friend, classmate, and colleague Rabbi Adam Feldman, *z"l*, delivered a Rosh Hashanah sermon to his congregation, The Princeton Jewish Center. The text on which Adam based his sermon was Louis Armstrong's famed "What a Wonderful World," a song whose lyrics prompt the listener to see the beauty and the blessings of our existence.

Adam explained to his congregation that the song topped the charts in 1968, a year that was anything but wonderful. The assassinations of Martin Luther King Jr. and Robert F. Kennedy, the riots at the Democratic National Convention, demonstrations against Vietnam – by any measure, 1968 was a difficult year, and yet the song . . . was a hit. Armstrong was criticized by members of the younger generation who bristled at lyrics that drew the listener's attention to "skies of blue" and "clouds of white" rather than the societal ills in need of redress.

Adam related that Armstrong eventually responded to his critics saying:

> "Some of you young folks have been saying to me, 'Hey, Pops, what do you mean, *What a wonderful world?* How about all them wars all over the place, you call them wonderful?' But how about listening to old Pops for a minute? Seems to me it ain't the world that's so bad but what we're doing to it, and all I'm saying is: see what a wonderful world it would be if only we'd give it a chance."

Armstrong's (and Adam's) point was that to focus on the wonder and beauty of the world in spite of its failings can prod us to seek to close the gap between the world as it is and the world as it ought to be. A person who is able to appreciate beauty in this world is filled not only with gratitude but also a sense of global stewardship, an insistence on working to make our deeply imperfect world a little more perfect. Last Rosh Hashanah, Adam preached to his community that when a Jew enters the synagogue, every day, but especially on Rosh Hashanah, we are obligated to give thanks for the blessings of our existence, and then, equally important, to commit to Tikkun Olam, mending our world that is in disrepair.

Ever since we were rabbinical school classmates, Adam and I would exchange sermon ideas, and I remember how moved I was last summer when he shared a draft of what would be his final Rosh Hashanah address. Since Adam's death, I have found myself returning to his words, trying to make sense of how to appreciate a world in which my friend could be taken so suddenly. I pray that Adam's wife Sara and children Talia, Dena, and Ilan find comfort in Adam's words as they face the monumental task of finding beauty in a world without their beloved husband and father.

Adam did not live to see a world turned upside down by the effects of COVID-19. As the sermons at the beginning of this volume make clear, our world did not lack for problems prior to the pandemic. Indeed, it is possible to read this year's collection of sermons as two volumes – the first, a reflection on our concerns prior to COVID and the second, an attempt to make sense of our world ever since. Our world is forever changed. We are coping daily, and the long-term impact of our present upheaval will not be fully understood for generations to come. If there was ever a time to lean into well-deserved pessimism, isn't that time now?

Which is why Adam's charge is more pressing than ever. In this uncertain hour, we must muster a sense of appreciation for our blessings – for our sake and for the sake of our children and grandchildren. We must commit to preserving and mending our world. For Jews, our sense of gratitude leads not to complacency but to an awareness of the fragility of the gift of life and our responsibility to protect it. Maybe it is precisely during a time that the world is decidedly not so wonderful that we need to nurture our sense of awe and wonder, inspiring us to engage in acts of generosity and compassion and in deeds of righteousness and justice.

I am heartbroken that I will not have my friend Adam to exchange sermon ideas with this summer and future summers, but I would like to think that were he here, it is the above message that he would counsel me to preach. It is to Rabbi Adam Feldman, *HaRav Avraham Tzvi ben Aryeh v'Ḥannah*, that I dedicate this volume.

The name of this year's volume of sermons comes from the final Torah reading of the book of Genesis, as Jacob blesses his grandsons, Joseph's sons, Ephraim and Manasseh. "Bring them close," Jacob instructs Joseph, "that I may bless them." (Genesis 48:9). What was for the aged Jacob a request for assistance has become for all future Jewish educators an abiding charge. What is the mission of every Jewish educator (and synagogue) if not the challenge and opportunity to bring Jews closer to tradition, community and God. I would be remiss if I did not also share that "Bring them close" is what Rabbi Neil Zuckerman (also Adam's classmate and friend) and I whisper to each other just before one of us takes the pulpit of Park Avenue Synagogue. "Bring them close" – the first and fundamental task of every rabbi.

Thank you, as always, to Jean Bloch Rosensaft and Rebecca Raphael Feuerstein for the many hours you have invested in the editorial process of this volume. To my colleague, editor, research aide, and muse, Marga Hirsch: Thank you for everything you do toward the production of this volume. I am, as always, filled with gratitude.

Elliot J. Cosgrove
July 2019
Tammuz 5780

Shof'tim 5779
Something to Say

Not once, not twice, not three times, but more times than I can count this past summer I was struck by the thought, *Thank God I am not preaching this Shabbat.* Summers at Park Avenue Synagogue, construction notwithstanding, are a delightfully quiet time. We move services out of the Sanctuary, our children go off to summer camp, the steady stream of bnei mitzvah takes a hiatus, and the clergy, both rabbis and cantors, take well-deserved down time. Should you be around during the summer, you should make a habit of coming to shul. It is one of the sweetest and most *heimish* times to be here: you get a nice davening, connection to community, and a cookie on your way home. No choir, no organ, no livestreaming . . . and no big sermons.

And because world events made the summer, well, the train wreck that it was, it was a relief to not have to preach every week. We had, and continue to have, an immigrant crisis at the border. There were shootings in Virginia Beach, El Paso, Dayton, and just last week, in Odessa, Texas. A climate crisis felt by all that is actively playing out in the Amazon. Trade wars, crises of democracy around the world, and stand-offs between nations. For Jews, things have not exactly been quiet either. Anti-Semitism – both at home and abroad – on the rise. A hot proxy war between Israel and Iran. A second Israeli election and a primary season in America that are bringing out the worst in all parties on both sides of the ocean. An American president counseling an Israeli prime minister to disallow US Congresswomen from entering Israel – a gut check for American Jewry the likes of which I have not experienced in my lifetime. It was an exchange made all the more testing by the presidential suggestion that any Jew who supports the Democratic party is disloyal to our country. The list goes on and on, one crisis snowballing into the next, and through it all, I said to myself, *Thank God I am not preaching this Shabbat.*

And now, the summer is over. And now, I have something to say.

The name of this morning's parashah is *Shof'tim*, which means "Judges." No surprise, the Torah reading begins with the commandment to Israel to appoint judges in all its territories in order "to govern the people with due justice." (Deuteronomy 16:18) But that is only the beginning. Our parashah is about far more than the judiciary and the principles by which it adjudicates law. While our nation has three branches of government, Ancient Israel was divided into four branches. First, as noted, the judiciary, which interestingly, as in the cases of Samson and Deborah, also came to include military leadership. Second, the monarchy, perhaps the most prestigious of the four authorities. Israel had an early form of constitutional monarchy: a powerful king subject to God's law, of which a copy was to sit literally at his side. Third, as a religious society based on sacrifices, Ancient Israel also had a priestly authority, leaders with oversight over matters of worship and cult, descending entirely from the tribe of Levi. The fourth and final authority, the one I want to focus on today, is the office of the prophet. *Navi mikirbekha . . . yakim l'kha*, "The Lord your God will raise up for you a prophet from among your people. . . ." (Deuteronomy 18:15) In the royal court or not, the prophet was the most important authority, the channel of communication to God. Part oracle, part healer, part messenger, the prophet was endowed with a divine intimacy, able to convey God's will, and most importantly, to serve a critical function vis-à-vis the three other authorities. As in the case of King David and the prophet Nathan, the prophet legitimized the monarchy or denounced its moral lapses and offenses. As in the case of Isaiah, the prophet corrected the excesses or oversights of the priests. The prophet was the ancient system of checks and balances, watching, naming, and when necessary, checking both the abuses of

Israel's leaders and the Israelites themselves when they violated the terms of the covenant. (J. Tigay, *JPS Torah Commentary: Deuteronomy*)

The prophet was all this and so much more. In his 1962 book *The Prophets*, Rabbi Abraham Joshua Heschel begins his study by asking the question "What manner of man is the prophet?" Heschel explains that the prophet is an individual willing to say "no" to his society, "condemning its habits and assumptions . . . [and] complacency." The prophet reminds Israel that "few are guilty, but all are responsible." The prophet is a warrior for morality, a champion contrarian, willing to go against the grain, refusing to be neutral in the face of evil even if it means, as is often the case, living a lonely and deeply unpopular life. Essentially, the prophet is the voice of dissent. And while the formal time of the prophets may have ended with the close of the Hebrew Bible, the prophetic voice continued to be a vital part of the project of Judaism. By this telling, prophecy is not located in any one person, class, or generation, but is an essential attribute, part of the DNA of the Jewish people. From the very first Jew, Abraham, arguing with God as the fate of Sodom and Gemorrah was at stake, through the time of the prophets, to Heschel himself, who fought on behalf of civil rights and protested the Vietnam War, it is the ability to take a moral stand, to refuse to let the abuses of an age become normalized that is the hallmark of our faith. As Heschel wrote: "Dissent is indigenous to Judaism." ("Dissent," in *Abraham Joshua Heschel: Essential Writings*, p. 106)

Our era does not lack for crises. At home, abroad, some self-inflicted and some, as in the devastation in the Bahamas, horrific acts of nature. I have my list; I am sure you have yours. But for me, the most terrifying crisis of all, the one that impacts every area of my concern, is that somehow, somewhere along the way we have lost our prophetic voice; we have lost the will to dissent. We have turned quiescent, morally timid, indifferent to the callings of the hour. For some, it is a matter of political expediency, for some a matter of self-interest, for some just plain laziness. So-and-so is good on Israel or the economy, and so we give a pass and fail to express outrage when our sense of decency is affronted. So-and-so is good on progressive causes, and so we refrain from condemning bald expressions of anti-Semitism. We shame people who dare voice an unpopular opinion, attacking their character instead of arguing the merits of their ideas, bullying them into silence. Jews who object to the Israeli government are marked as self-hating Zionists and Jews. Jews who object to the present administration are labeled disloyal and unpatriotic. The causes are manifold, but the effect is one and the same: We are forsaking the birthright of our prophetic voice. I think of a comment Martin Luther King made on his era: "History will . . . record that the greatest tragedy of this period of social transition was not the strident clamor of the bad people, but the appalling silence of the good people." We have lost the mojo that makes Jews . . . Jews.

And it is not, mind you, only as Jews that our self-audit proves lacking; it is also as Americans. You can tell the tale of our country in a variety of ways – as God's New Israel, as a melting pot of immigrants, and otherwise – but as the historian Robert Young writes: "Protest is one of the consummate expressions of 'Americanness.'" Even before our nation was established, religious dissent was the calling card of the English colonies. It was rebellion that led to the birth of our nation. It was the steady stream of dissenters who demanded the abolition of slavery, suffrage for women, rights for Native Americans, for Latinos, for African Americans, reproductive rights, and gay rights. From the Puritans to protests against the Patriot act, from the anthems of Pete Seeger to Zucotti Park, it is the radicals, reformers, reactionaries, and revolutionaries who have made this nation the great nation that it is. And I would be remiss if I failed to point out that dissent has many faces – some that may not reflect the liberal leanings of the Upper East Side. The Tea Party and Religious Right also understand themselves as counterctultural dissenters in the classical sense. And then of course there is the delicate question of the means we employ to give our dissent expression. Be it John Brown at Harper's Ferry, Henry David Thoreau at Walden or Martin Luther King in the Birmingham jail, the question of when and how one breaks an unjust law in order to serve a higher law is a question deserving of careful inquiry. (R. Young, *Dissent: The History of an American Idea*)

But to stay silent? To not say anything? That is something that, as Americans and as Jews, we cannot, dare not, and will not do – not anywhere, and especially not here in the synagogue. As a mentor of mine once taught me: the function of a house of worship is to "comfort the afflicted and afflict the comfortable." In our era where the political and business communities seem more and more disinclined to object to the outrages of the day, it is increasingly incumbent upon the religious community, this religious community, to take up the prophetic mantle that is our patrimony. Yes, we enter this room for sanctuary, both literally and figuratively. Yes, the first obligation of a synagogue is to bring people closer to Torah, to tradition and community – to be an incubator of Jewish identity. But as I have said many times from this very spot, we come to synagogue not to hear about the world as it is, but as it ought to be. We come to synagogue to be reminded that the task of creation is not yet complete and that we are partners with God in repairing a deeply fractured world. We come to synagogue to be challenged, to hear the prophetic voice of our tradition, and to be inspired to find our own prophetic voice. The social contract of a synagogue is not that we will all agree with everything that is said here – on the pulpit or in the pews. The social contract of the synagogue is that we will leave here knowing better what our tradition says about the issues of the day and motivated to engage respectfully with those whose views differ from our own.

As Jews and as Americans, it is neither unpatriotic nor disloyal to voice dissent, regarding our government or the government of Israel. If there is one message of these weeks leading up to the High Holidays, it is that criticism and love are not opposites but two sides of the same coin. Whether it concerns our family, our country, or the State of Israel, to voice dissent from a place of love is arguably the most Jewish, most loyal, most Zionist, and most important thing an American Jew can do.

Tzedek, tzedek tirdof. Justice, justice thou shalt pursue. (Deuteronomy 16:20) Famously, the rabbis ask why the word *tzedek*, justice, is stated twice. Once would have been enough. Of the many explanations, I find myself moved by the thought that the pursuit of justice is twofold: *tzedek* when it is easy, and *tzedek* when it is hard; *tzedek* both when it is convenient and *tzedek* when, perhaps especially when, it is inconvenient – when we have something to lose. Friends, summer is over. It is time we say something. More importantly, it is time we do something.

September 7, 2019
7 Elul 5779

Nitzavim 5779
Say It Ain't So, Joe

To the degree that American sports culture bears the stain of an original sin, this month marks the one hundredth anniversary of the felonious offense. In the final week of September 1919, on the Upper West Side of New York, a group of White Sox ballplayers met to throw the upcoming World Series against the Cincinnati Reds. The details of the fix and the eight members of the conspiring "Black Sox" who accepted money from gamblers, are best documented in Eliot Asinof's book (and subsequent movie): *Eight Men Out*. But more than the facts of the case, it is the mythic status that the Black Sox scandal has acquired that has come to loom over the American psyche. Reference is made, among other places, in F. Scott Fitzgerald's *The Great Gatsby*, as well as by Hyman Roth of "Godfather" fame, who attributed his love of baseball to "Arnold Rothstein who fixed the World Series." Bernard Malamud's famous novel and subsequent movie *The Natural* borrows historic elements from the scandal. Kevin Costner's "Field of Dreams" affirmed the story for my generation, and most recently, Major League Baseball announced an August 2020 regular season game to be played between the Yankees and White Sox in those iconic Iowa cornfields. Whether or not a child ever actually said, "Say it ain't so, Joe," to Shoeless Joe Jackson outside the courthouse (which no child did), is beside the point. It is the moral subtext beneath the events of one hundred years ago, the fall from grace of our heroes, that, from generation to generation, continues to play an outsized role in the moral imagination of our country.

Given the anniversary, given that tomorrow night is Rosh Hashanah, given that we are on the eve of both the pennant race and the penitential season, this morning I want to give a different sort of a sermon. A warm-up of sorts. I want to use the centennial anniversary of the Black Sox scandal as a portal into the subject matter of the season: sin, forgiveness, and the human condition. A moral clinic, if you will, for all the themes that we should be considering in the days ahead.

First, and most obviously: sin. To study the Black Sox scandal is to do a deep dive into the nature of sin. The most striking thing I noticed in every treatment of the scandal was an implicit or explicit gesture towards justifying the actions of the players. The White Sox owner, Charles Comiskey, was miserly. He underpaid his players and got rich off their talents. Who could blame the players for trying to make some extra cash? Alternatively, some reasoned, the eight players who were on the take were just doing what everybody was doing. The Black Sox scandal was neither the first, nor for that matter, the last such scandal. As ringleader Charles "Swede" Risberg revealed years later, there had been four prior rigged games in 1917 between the White Sox and the Tigers that everybody knew about. The World Series may have been a difference in degree but not in kind; those eight players were just following standard practice.

Such arguments are not new. Ever since Adam blamed Eve in the Garden of Eden, people have sought to deflect their own failings.

"Me speeding, officer? I was only keeping up with the flow of traffic! I am doing nothing that everybody else isn't doing."

"Everyone is using performance enhancing drugs. I'm getting my edge no differently than everyone else!"

"Our marriage has been on the rocks for years; am I really the one to blame?"

We say to ourselves, "just this once," which becomes twice, which becomes normalized, and then not a sin at all. It was one of my predecessors, Rabbi Milton Steinberg, who wrote a sermon entitled "Only Human: The Eternal Alibi." We look back on the year gone by knowing we are masterful moral contortionists. We blame others, we blame the world in which we live, most often we blame our own humanity. We blame anyone or anything to avoid taking responsibility for our actions.

All of which, while fully understandable, is totally contrary to the central premise of the imminent holiday season. The basis of Jewish ethics is that as human beings we have moral agency. For Jews, being human is not an alibi; being human is a call to action – the insistence that we set the moral bar high and believe ourselves capable of grabbing onto it. Nobody is hardwired one way or another. Yes, sometimes we make good choices, sometimes we make bad choices, but that ability to choose – that is what makes us human. Yom Kippur wouldn't make any sense if we didn't believe we had free will, that we can repent our past and choose a new course of action. Of course, our world is filled with temptation and corrupting influences, and sin is ever crouching at our door. The days ahead throw down a bold challenge to our humanity: that we can avoid the moral trip wires that abound and rise to our God-given potential.

Second: To study the Black Sox scandal is to wrestle with the dynamics of forgiveness. I imagine in the weeks ahead there will be plenty of retrospectives about the scandal, and I am willing to bet (excuse the expression), that there will be more ink spilled on the irrevocable ban the players received than on the offense itself. To his dying day, third baseman Buck Weaver sought to clear his name and be reinstated to baseball – a campaign that his descendants have continued. Guilty or not, the question stands: Was it fair, was it just, to ban these players for life? Why do athletes found guilty of cheating by taking steroids receive a temporary suspension, but those found guilty of gambling are declared permanently ineligible and beyond redemption? It has been years since I have been to the Hall of Fame in Cooperstown, but I've heard that visitors can now vote on whether or not Pete Rose should be allowed into the Hall of Fame. How does one measure the gravity of sin? How does one determine the proportionality of punishment? And if, as we would all hopefully allow, people are capable of remorse and repentance, then how do we determine when forgiveness is merited?

The dynamics surrounding these questions are very delicate and I want to tread very, very carefully, certainly in a sermon wedged into the day before Rosh Hashanah. We should all be grateful that we live in an age where people's misdeeds are no longer brushed under the rug, where individuals are held publicly accountable for their offenses, where the veneer of their power, celebrity, gender, or religious leadership provides no protection against their reprehensible behavior: football players, opera singers, and prime ministers, to name but a few from last week's news cycle. And no question, there are sins and sinners that are beyond redemption, disqualified from re-entering polite society. But what about the more quotidian provinces of our lives? The friend who let you down, the co-worker who broke a confidence, the family member who fell short of expectation. Do they stay benched forever? If someone has expressed remorse and paid their debt, then when exactly do they get another swing at the plate? The corollary to the belief that the consequence of free will is the possibility of poor choices, is the possibility that free will can result in good choices, in self-correction, in being proven worthy of forgiveness. It would be no small thing if members of this community were to spend these next days considering people we have wronged and seeking their forgiveness. But what would be even more impressive would be if we spent these coming days considering those individuals who seek our forgiveness and then . . . if we granted it. We would enter the new year having lightened their burden, and, more likely, having lightened our own.

Third and finally – and I don't know how to say this in legalese, but I imagine one of the eight hundred attorneys in this room can – is the line, brought into relief by the Black Sox scandal, between guilt and responsibility. As you may know, just shy of two years after the thrown World Series, all eight players were acquitted of criminal charges. But a day after their acquittal, baseball Commissioner Kenesaw Mountain Landis ruled that the players, nevertheless, would be banned for life. His stated reasoning was that regardless of the verdict of the prior day, "No player that sits in a conference with a bunch of crooked players and gamblers where the ways and means of throwing games are planned and discussed and does not promptly tell his club about it, will ever play professional baseball." For Landis, the moral bar was much higher than whether a player did or didn't participate in the fix. It was the mere knowledge of wrongdoing – knowledge and failure to report or take action – that was also an egregious breach of trust, egregious enough to disqualify a player from ever playing again in America's national pastime.

In the coming days, as we assess not only our own condition, but the condition of our world and our obligations within it; it is on this measure that we know we fall painfully short. As Rabbi Abraham Joshua Heschel taught: "In a free society, some are guilty, but all are responsible." Willful ignorance abounds – take your pick from the headlines: CEOs of car companies, of e-cigarette companies; in the private sector, in government, in our own Jewish community. Ours is an age in need of more, not fewer, whistleblowers. What does it say about the moral condition of our age when a four-star general invokes *devoir de réserve*, the duty of silence, to justify his moral acquiescence to misdeeds around him, and a sixteen-year-old girl is the one who is courageously speaking truth to power regarding the climate crisis? This morning's Torah reading warns us of the danger of fancying ourselves immune, thinking, "I shall be safe. . . ." (Deuteronomy 29:18), believing ourselves to be innocent just because we are not guilty. As Jews we answer to a higher authority; it is not enough to merely wonder if we are guilty of wrongdoing. In the days ahead, it will be sins of both commission and omission for which we must account, one of which we know to be the failure to speak out. It is both our action and inaction by which we are measured. We are all responsible. We are all moral contributors to the world in which we live.

Sin, forgiveness, the obligation to speak out. The shadow of the Black Sox scandal continues to loom because it is a morality tale containing the fundamental questions confronting the human condition. In the immortal words of James Earl Jones, baseball reminds us "of all that once was good and that could be again." Who doesn't want to be taken out to the ball game? Isn't that what the High Holidays are also all about? A reminder of all that once was good and that could be again – for us, for our families, and for our country.

Warm-up is over. Tomorrow night, 6:00 pm, here in this sanctuary, our fall classic begins. Play ball!

September 28, 2019
28 Elul 5779

Erev Rosh Hashanah 5780
Angels in Hardhats

If our synagogue's present construction serves as any indication, then on that first Shabbat of Creation, when the good Lord stepped back to behold the divine handiwork, the wi-fi was nowhere near close to being hooked up. Printers had not been connected to the mainframe; furniture was sitting in a shipping container on a dock in New Jersey; and some angel had forgotten to install a phone jack in God's office. Why did God wait until the fifth day to fill the land, sea, and air with living creatures? Now I know. Because the angel entrusted to supply the TCO, the Temporary Certificate of Occupancy, chose that week – of all weeks – to go on vacation!

Park Avenue Synagogue: Welcome back to 87th Street! As staff, we re-entered the building on September 4, but I imagine that for most of you, this evening – Rosh Hashanah – is your first time back to behold all the progress . . . and all that is still in progress. As I have reflected many times from this bimah, it is of deep significance that when the world was established, the adjective God used to describe creation was *tov*, "good," not "perfect," not "flawless," and certainly not "complete." There is still work to be done, details to attend to, and we are all looking forward to the formal dedication on Sunday, December 8. But even now, it is incumbent upon us to pause, to note how far we have come, and to appreciate all that *is tov*, all that *is* good. To say "thank you" to you, our members, for your shared vision, support, and patience. And while the entire leadership under our Chairman Marc Becker and President Natalie Barth deserves thanks,

I would be remiss if I did not publicly express gratitude to the synagogue officer who has shepherded the construction every day, every step of the way – the indefatigable, the one-and-only Craig Solomon.

Having never lived through a building project of this magnitude, I naively believed that the sequencing of a construction project was a fairly straightforward undertaking. Construction is announced, construction is completed, and construction is enjoyed. What I have discovered, what everyone else seemed to know but never told me, is that nothing could be further from the truth. Construction is messy, punch lists take time to complete, and the act of creation extends well beyond the date of occupancy.

In fact, as the rabbis tell it, far from a crisply sequenced undertaking, the creation of our world itself – what Rosh Hashanah commemorates – was a similarly frenetic deadline-busting effort. *Pirkei Avot*, the Ethics of Our Fathers, relates the anxious hours prior to that first Shabbat – corresponding to our precise moment, theologically speaking – when God remembered a list of ten items that had been overlooked. (5:8) Ten things that had to be rush ordered at twilight – including the rainbow to follow the Flood, the manna to sustain the Israelites through their desert wanderings, and the tablets upon which the Ten Commandments would be engraved. What a great image, one that I hope gives our Executive Director Beryl Chernov comfort – that even God had to yell at the foreman to get the job done by deadline.

As I researched these *midrashim*, these rabbinic glosses to the Genesis story, I discovered that there are actually different lists scattered throughout rabbinic literature describing different things that God created prior to Creation, including, for instance, the Torah, the Holy Temple, and God's throne of glory. But of all the things on all the lists of what needed to be created prior to the physical universe coming into being, the most remarkable, the most curious, and the most relevant for our purposes today is not actually a "thing" at all, but an idea, a concept or behavior. And that is *teshuvah*, repentance. *Teshuvah*, repentance, stands alone, an idea without which the world itself would not and could not exist.

So, I began to wonder why. Why would God need to create *teshuvah* as a precondition to creation? The first answer, I think, requires knowledge of another midrash, which teaches that God had actually created other worlds prior to this one, but each one disappointed; none of them worked out. What was missing in these earlier creations? What was missing was the one thing we all know is needed in order to handle our world's inevitable disappointments, setbacks, and shortcomings. The ability to see beyond a slight, to see the big picture, and to move forward: *teshuvah*. Only before our present world was created did God finally understand that in order for this world or any world to endure, it would need some give. It would need to forgive. Like a skyscraper built to sway in the event of an earthquake, *teshuvah* was the "give" built into the world in order to withstand the inevitable imperfections to come.

It is a sweet thought, but it lacks precision, because strictly speaking, *teshuvah* does not mean forgiveness; *teshuvah* means repentance. Namely, the ability of an individual to reflect on the past, to feel remorse over one's behavior, and to resolve to choose a new course of action in the future. By this thinking, *teshuvah* had to exist prior to Creation, because it is the precondition not just to our world, but to our very humanity. As the great sage Maimonides taught, our humanity is based on two fundamental theses. First, that every human being is endowed with the ability to distinguish between good and bad; and second, that every human being is endowed with the ability to choose between good and bad. Simply put, without *teshuvah*, without moral agency, human beings would not be human.

It is this idea that *teshuvah* is what makes us human that is the premise behind the High Holidays – the theological ante, if you will, to the days ahead. Rosh Hashanah and Yom Kippur wouldn't make any sense if we didn't believe we had free will, that we can repent our past and choose a new course of action. This evening we commit to shedding all the excuses we employ year-round to justify our behavior: that we were "just doing what everyone else is doing," that "circumstances were beyond our control," and that ownerless "mistakes were made." To believe in *teshuvah* means that we look back on the year knowing that we *did* know better, we *did* have the choice, and, nevertheless, we made bad choices. All the rationalizations, deflections, and justifications – all of them – are checked at the door tonight. There is another midrash that teaches that when a child is conceived, an angel brings the fetus before God. The angel asks, "Will this child be tall or short?" God decrees its height. "Will this child be smart or not?" God decrees its intellectual capacity. Then the angel asks, "Will this child be good or bad?" And God is silent. Because moral volition is not a matter of divine decree but of individual choice. To believe in *teshuvah* is a bold challenge to our humanity – because it means that our mistakes belong to nobody but ourselves. But it also means that we can, if we so choose, rise to our God-given potential.

And that still isn't the full picture. The formation of *teshuvah* at Creation is not just about God, nor, for that matter, just about you and me. *Teshuvah* is actually about other people, or more precisely, about all of us. Because if you believe, if you truly believe, that you and I can be reflective and remorseful and change for the better – then you know what? That person who wronged you in the year gone by: you have to believe that he or she can change, too! The person who caused you hurt, the one who demonstrated such poor judgment, the person whom you have benched indefinitely from your life – that person is also capable of reflection; that person is also capable of regret; that person is also capable of course correction; and that person may just be worthy of forgiveness.

One of the most enigmatic *midrashim* regarding Creation tells of God deciding to create humanity while the ministering angels debated over whether humankind should be created. Love said: "Let them be created for they will do loving deeds." Truth said: "Let them not be created because they will fall short of truth." Righteousness said: "Let them be created because they will do righteous deeds." Peace said, "Let them not be created because they will bring discord." On and on they debated, right in front of God, the midrash teaches, until God seized hold of Truth and threw it upon the earth, thus creating the first human. (*Bereshit Rabbah* 8:5)

I will be the first to admit that I don't fully understand the text. But I think part of its message is that in order for humanity to be created, Truth had to be thrown to the ground, lest any one human claim to be in possession of Truth in its entirety. None of us are in possession of the whole truth; there is always another side of the story, and during the days ahead we need to be open to hearing it. I am well aware that I personally have caused people hurt this past year. When I know, I reach out: I call, I email, I write a note, I ask someone out for coffee, I do whatever I can to seek forgiveness. When someone reaches out to tell me that I let them down, that I caused them offense, I try my best to resist the urge to be defensive. I remind myself that there is always another side. I don't know if in the days ahead we will resolve all the hurts of the year gone by – that is a tall order. But I do know that if we fail to allow for the possibility that none of us is in possession of the whole truth, if we fail to allow for the possibility that our loved ones are as capable of change as we would like to think we ourselves are, then this entire season of repentance will not amount to very much.

I imagine there are all sorts of reasons why *teshuvah* had to be built into Creation, why it was a precondition to the existence of our world. It's the sort of question we should all be thinking about during the holidays. But it was sometime last week, as I was writing late at night in my new office (with the Wi-Fi now up and running), that it finally hit me. I had gotten up to stretch, and I took a stroll through the building. I saw all the construction workers and maintenance professionals working round the clock and through the night, these angels in hardhats, working furiously to put our building back together. Not a new building, but a return to our old one, returned not to its former glory, but to a beauty beyond what anyone imagined possible. A building that honors all that came before and is poised to house an infinite number of memories still yet to come.

And I thought to myself, *if that isn't what these High Holidays are all about, then I don't know what is*. And I remembered that the word *teshuvah* doesn't just mean repentance; the word *teshuvah*, from the

Hebrew root *shuv*, means "returning." *Teshuvah* signals the possibility of a return home *and* the promise of a new future – at one and the same time.

Why did God establish *teshuvah* at the twilight of Creation? Because God wanted us to be able to feel like we felt when we re-entered this building this evening. A feeling of coming home hand-in-hand with the experience of something altogether new, the familiar mixed with the unfamiliar, the sense of comfort alongside the thrill of the unknown; in other words, the sensation that we are entering into a new chapter of our lives. That is what *teshuvah* feels like. That is what these High Holidays are about. And that is why God had to create *teshuvah* before our world came into existence. God knew that over the course of our lives we would wander and go astray, and so God gave us the divine gift of *teshuvah*, of return, of finding our way back home, even as we step forward into new territory. That is the promise of this building, that is the promise of these High Holidays.

Friends, welcome back to 87th Street. It is beautiful, it is new, it is *tov*. It is *tov m'od*, very good – and it is your home. This is the place where you belong. A new building. A new year. Let's make the most of it!

September 29, 2019
29 Elul 5779

Rosh Hashanah 5780
If Not Now, Then When?

Let me tell you, it's never been easy to be the rabbi of Park Avenue Synagogue, beginning with our founding rabbi, Edward Benjamin Morris Browne. Hungarian-born, fluent in six languages, Rabbi Browne was known as "Alphabet Browne" due to his penchant for signing his name with the letters of all his degrees (LLD, AM, BM, DD, MD). In the 1880s, he was the rabbi of Congregation Gates of Hope, which merged in 1882 with Agudat Yesharim, which became the congregation you and I know as Park Avenue Synagogue.

In addition to his leadership of our community at its founding, Rabbi Browne was a friend of Ulysses S. Grant, General of the Union Army and eighteenth president of the United States. Rabbi Browne visited Grant regularly as his health declined and, on the Shabbat of Grant's passing in 1885, declared from the pulpit: "The Jews have lost a great friend in the death of General Grant." Browne elevated Grant's stature even above that of Moses, proclaiming: "Moses liberated 3,000,000 of people, his own brethren, from Egyptian bondage. Grant liberated 3,000,000 of people, a race not his own, from American bondage," and concluded with the call for the entire congregation to rise to recite kaddish. Not surprisingly, Rabbi Browne was asked to be an honorary pallbearer at the funeral set to take place in New York City. (Jonathan Sarna, *When General Grant Expelled the Jews*, p. 139)

Rabbi Browne's unrestrained outpouring of grief for Grant was far from a given among American Jews. Grant, a Republican, was not an uncontroversial figure. His personal life was marked by excess and indulgence; his business record, checkered; he was elected president despite lacking prior political experience; and his leadership was marked by political and economic scandal, a legacy that continues to be debated to this day. For American Jews, Grant was forever dishonored for his having signed General Orders No. 11, "the most notorious anti-Jewish official order in American history," issued in 1862 during the Civil War. In a story best told by historian Dr. Jonathan Sarna, Grant called for the expulsion of "Jews as a class" from Tennessee, Mississippi, and Kentucky. In the eyes of many Jews, Grant's infamous decree, though quickly rolled back by Lincoln, forever labeled him an enemy of our people.

Things came to a head in the election of 1868. Browne's former mentor, the nationally renowned Rabbi Isaac Mayer Wise, was a dyed-in-the-wool Democrat and fierce critic of abolitionists and their repeated use of antisemitic rhetoric and tropes. Wise believed that the cause of African Americans came at the expense of American Jewry and that to vote for Grant was a betrayal of Jewish self-interest. (p. 55) Others, such as Louisville attorney Louis N. Dembitz, uncle to the future Justice, sought to rehabilitate Grant, believing that Grant's efforts on behalf of reconstruction more than mitigated his earlier anti-Jewish missteps and the latent antisemitism of progressives. (p. 60) Besides, as Rabbi Liebman Adler, rabbi of Chicago's oldest synagogue would argue, American Jews must vote not as Jews but as American citizens. In Adler's words: "If the party in whose hands I believe the welfare of the country . . . was the safest, were to place a Haman at the helm of state, and the opposite party, whose non-existence I believe would be better for . . . my country, were to place [the] Messiah at their head . . . Moses the Chief Justice, and . . . the Patriarchs to the cabinet, I should say, 'Prosper under Haman, my fatherland, and here you have my vote, even if all the Jew in me mourns.'"(p. 74)

American Jews faced a conundrum. There were Jews who believed, as Jews, that their priority must be their parochial well-being. There were also Jews who believed, as Jews, that they were obligated to prioritize the progressive Republican agenda over their own. Should a Jew vote for a party he or she considers bad for the country to avoid voting for a person perceived to be bad for the Jews? Should a Jew prioritize the progressive agenda if doing so runs contrary to Jewish self-interest? What is the self-interest of the Jewish community anyway and who gets to decide?

Grant was elected in 1868 and then again in 1872, but his leadership continued to split American Jewry. Whether due to pragmatism, principle, or penance, Grant's administration included more Jews than any of his predecessors. Grant intervened to assist Jews abroad facing persecution and pogroms, making the unprecedented decision to appoint a Jewish consul to Romania. Grant was the first president to attend a synagogue dedication – all three hours of it! Post-presidency, Grant was the first American president to set foot in Jerusalem. By many metrics Grant was good for the Jews; by others, no way. American Jewry was fiercely divided over what their Judaism called on them to do.

So you can only imagine the stir it caused when my predecessor was called on to serve as one of the honorary pallbearers at Grant's funeral. In addition to Grant's disputed legacy among Jews, and in addition to other New York rabbis being annoyed that Browne, rabbi of an upstart uptown synagogue, was picked to represent all of American Jewry, there was the small matter that the day of the funeral, August 8, 1885, fell on Shabbat. Reform rabbi though he was, Browne was a traditionalist at heart, a proud Jew and opponent of the then-movement to shift Shabbat to Sunday. On that day, representing all Jews, there was no way that Browne would ride in a carriage and break Shabbat. Browne's congregation, like American Jewry as a whole, was split. Like most rabbis, Browne didn't mind the limelight; like most rabbis, Browne didn't mind having a job. Should he or shouldn't he participate in the funeral procession? What, oh what, would our founding rabbi decide to do? (J. Rothschild Blumberg, *Prophet in a Time of Priests: Rabbi "Alphabet" Browne 1845-1929*)

But before I tell you . . . Happy New Year! *Shanah Tovah* to each and every one of you! Today is Rosh Hashanah, our new year, our annual check-in and checkup, the day we are instructed to take the pulse of the Jewish people, reflect on our place within our wider humanity and the roles we must play in order to strengthen our people and our world in the year ahead. The headlines, we know, are not good, not for the world and not for the Jews. We have had a year of environmental crises, a year of gun violence, a year of refugees across the globe and at our own border. A year of rising antisemitism, with violent attacks in Pittsburgh, Poway, Brooklyn, Europe, and elsewhere. A year of a progressive left increasingly inhospitable to the pro-Israel community and the Jewish community. Another year of conflict for Israel: a proxy war with Iran and the prospects of peace between Israel and her neighbors, a two-state solution, as elusive as ever. Impeachment proceedings just announced. Not one, but two elections in Israel (and maybe a third), which, whatever the outcome, have served to spotlight the growing divide between American Jewry and Israel.

We do not lack for crises. We all have our lists of real problems, global and local, increasing in intensity. And our Jewish community stands in the midst of the whirlwind, Jew pitted against Jew, our already small community fractured further over the question of what is in the best interest of our people. There are Jews who believe, as Jews, that they must express outrage at the erosion of progressive values, who are demanding, as Jews, that we redouble our liberal commitments to mend the world, in America, around the globe, and Israel. And there are other Jews who believe, as Jews, that the aforementioned Jews are delusional, that those progressives are no friends to Jews. As Jews, our concern is the security and safety of the half of our people who reside in the Jewish state. It is the self-interest of our people, not the environment, gun control, the right to choose, the composition of the Supreme Court, or anything else that must be our priority. And because ours is a chilling era of intersectional politics, ideological purity, and public shaming, we have lost the ability to do the one thing that Jews across the spectrum have always prided themselves on doing: talk to each other – in our politics, within our communities, and even around our dinner tables. We call each other out as self-hating or disloyal, questioning each other's allegiance. An ugly schism in our ranks that has spilled into public view. And at the core of it all, no different than in the time of Rabbi Browne, is the question of defining Jewish interest. What exactly, as Jews, are we called on to do? If we believe something or someone to be good for the Jews but bad for the country, or bad for the Jews but good for the country, which takes priority, which gives way to which? Us or them? The particular or the universal? Given the imperfect choices available, which path shall we choose?

As long as Jews have been Jews, this struggle to order our priorities toward ourselves and toward others has shaped the contours of our being. When Abraham was first called on by God, his charge was two-fold: On the one hand: *lekh l'kha*, go to the promised land, a specific promise for a chosen people with a unique destiny. On the other hand: *v'heye brakhah*, "and you shall be a blessing" – you will be a blessing to all the nations of the earth. In our Torah reading for Rosh Hashanah, Sarah, fearing for the safety of her child, prioritizes her household and casts out Hagar, only for Hagar to be saved by God from certain death. The Exodus from Egypt, our particular story of national redemption, is also the story that reminds us to care for the stranger for we were once strangers in a strange land. And consider today's very celebration: Rosh Hashanah. *Hayom harat olam*, "today the world was created." Not the first Jew, but the first human, the ancestor of collective humanity. But we also have another new year, in Nissan, the month of Passover, commemorating the birth of the Jewish nation and the beginnings of peoplehood. Our parochial commitments are affirmed alongside our universal ones today and every day of the year. This is the dialectical tension embedded in every Jewish soul since our very beginning.

Some call it a tension, some a contradiction, some . . . a hyphen. Call it what you will, it is this concomitant commitment to our universal imperatives and particularistic responsibilities that is the double helix and defining strength of Jewish DNA. It is what inspired some Jews in the 1880s to come to our country's teeming shores inspired by the vision of Emma Lazarus, and other Jews, during the same years, to go to the shores of Palestine, inspired by the Zionist vision of Leon Pinsker. It is why 1948 marks not just the declaration of the State of Israel, but also the Universal Declaration of Human Rights, both drafted by Jews. It is why every organization committed to civil rights over the last 100 years – the ACLU, Amnesty International, the NAACP – has had a Jew in the room at its founding. (J. Loeffler, *Rooted Cosmopolitans: Jews and Human Rights in the Twentieth Century*) This is the secret sauce of our people – concern for ourselves and concern for others. Nobody put it better than our great sage Hillel, who himself lived during a time of social upheaval as Jews had to prioritize their commitments to themselves and their obligations to the world around. Some people love to quote the first part of Hillel's famed aphorism: *Im ein ani li, mi li?* "If I am not for myself, then who will be for me?" Some people love to quote the second part: *U-k'sheh-ani l'atzmi, mah ani?* "If I am only for myself, then what am I?" Both groups are wrong. To be a Jew is not one or the other, but both, or more directly, it is the pause, the breath we take between the two statements. *Amor Mundi* (Love of Humanity) alongside *Ahavat Yisrael* (Love of Israel) – this duality is the core of our Jewish self-understanding.

This year I seem to have arrived at the disorienting and undoubtedly fleeting state of seeing my children actually living the values that I have been drilling into them throughout their lives. One daughter is in Israel for a gap year before arriving at the other promised land of Ann Arbor, Michigan. Another daughter has taken on a more observant Jewish life, taping the light of the refrigerator to the "on" position over Shabbat, double-checking the kashrut of everything brought into our home, and davening . . . well . . . a lot. I am reminded of what my father said to me when I told him I wanted to be a rabbi: "Elliot, you know we always wanted you to be a proud Jew. We just never thought you would take us so seriously." My son, at least for the time being, is darn near perfect. But it was my second daughter, the one presently applying to college, who caught me off guard the other week. We were sitting in the college counselor's office, reviewing "the likelies," "the targets," and "the reaches," when my daughter straightened up, lifted her head, and said: "We are forgetting one option: that I make *aliyah* and join the IDF." Talk about "be careful what you ask for!" The look on the college counselor's face was priceless – probably mine too. Shall my daughter direct her passions to pursue a humanities degree on a liberal college campus, or lean into Jewish history by defending the Jewish state? She is torn, I am torn, and it doesn't help that the Zuckerman kid just made *aliyah*. I have no idea how her story will turn out. But I will tell you this: I am proud, deeply proud. I am proud of her struggle; I am proud she is torn; and I am proud to have both voices in her head and at my dinner table.

My concern, in a sentence, is that we have lost our ability to countenance, embrace, and take pride in the dual aspect of what it means to be an American Jew. Somewhere along the way, this very strength of ours has been turned against us – by us. We have forgotten that the Jews demonstrating on behalf of the environment, the Jews protesting what is happening at our borders – the Jews acting as Jews in the name of our Jewish values – they are us and we are them, and we should be proud of them and support them. We have also forgotten that the Jews fighting for the safety and security of our people, at home and abroad – they are also us and we are also them and we should be proud of them and support them and the values they are acting on. We need Jewish Democrats outraged by antisemitism emanating from the left just as we need Jewish Republicans outraged by antisemitism coming from the right. We need Jews in all camps, in positions of leadership, correcting the abuses and excesses on both sides. Most of all, we need Jews who refuse to let the world make us choose between the universal and the particular. We need Jews willing to stand proudly – as Jews – on behalf of our people and our shared humanity.

So what, some of you may still be wondering, did Rabbi Browne decide?

Initially, Browne requested that he be allowed to walk and not ride in the procession – a request that was refused. But given the friendship, the Grant family interceded and gave Browne special dispensation to "foot it," which is exactly what Browne did – all seven-and-a-half miles from City Hall to Riverside Park – with the whole city watching. Not surprisingly, the Jewish community, including this community was divided. Some lauded Browne for having honored Grant and the Sabbath. Others excoriated him for having participated in the procession at all.

But something else also happened on that fateful day as Browne walked the length of Manhattan. Browne's public display of his faith and patriotism – his picture on the front pages – caught the imagination of the public, who sat up and took note of this Jew who embraced and affirmed his people and his country, the particular and the universal at one and the same time. It was something that nobody, of any background, thought could be done. What Browne did wasn't important just for him or, for that matter, American Jewry. What Browne did that day was important for an America that didn't know it was possible to be loyal to one's faith and one's nation, one's kinsman and one's countryman, at one and the same time. America desperately needed a model of how to negotiate the multiple and often competing loyalties tearing away at its soul, and on that day, it was a Jew, our rabbi, Rabbi Browne, who provided the model for all Americans.

Which is basically what Rabbi Browne's great-granddaughter told me when I spoke to her this past summer. Janice Rothschild Blumberg is not just the great granddaughter of Rabbi Browne, she is also the rebbetzin of the late Rabbi Jacob Rothschild, rabbi of The Temple in Atlanta (of "Driving Miss Daisy" fame), the one that was bombed by the Ku Klux Klan in 1958 due to her husband's friendship with Martin Luther King Jr. and outspoken leadership in the civil rights movement. At 95 years old, the rebbetzin is sharp as a tack, regaling me not just with her views on Israeli politics, but with stories of her great-grandfather. My favorite is her telling of a game they played when she was a little girl. She would jump repeatedly into his arms to be caught, until he didn't catch her, and he said: "Now you know never to trust a Hungarian – even if it is your own great-grandfather." With her permission, I would like to share with you her reflections on Rabbi Browne's decision and the enduring legacy of her great-grandfather.

The rebbetzin told me that all American rabbis and for that matter, all American Jews, are asked to choose between being a proud Jew and being a proud citizen, between their faith and their patriotism, between their particular commitments and their universal ones. Rabbi Browne was asked to choose, just as the rebbetzin's late husband, Rabbi Rothschild, proud Zionist and proud advocate for civil rights, was told, by way of a bomb, that he had to choose. Every Jewish generation is told that they can't have it both ways. The legacy of Rabbi Browne was that he rejected the choice, or, more precisely, chose both. He took a stand and walked the seven and a half miles to punctuate the point. After all, the most important part of Hillel's aphorism is not the first part – "If I am not for myself"– and it is not the second part – "If am only for myself" – nor for that matter is it the breath between the two. The most important part of Hillel's aphorism is how it ends: *V'im lo aḥshav, eimatai?* "And if not now, then when?" The enduring lesson of Rabbi Browne is that he refused to sit on his hands and do nothing. He took his commitments to his faith, to his country, to his people, and to his shared humanity, and he wore them all proudly for all the world, and people of all backgrounds, to see.

That is the legacy of Rabbi Browne, and that is the DNA of this community; that is what it means to be an American Jew, and that is the calling of the hour. The stakes are too high, on too many fronts, for any of us to sit this round out. When you walk into this synagogue, you may hear a sermon about the threat of antisemitism and you may hear a sermon about the threat of climate change; you may be asked to mobilize on behalf of Israel's defense; and you may be asked to mobilize regarding the humanitarian crisis at our borders – and you should be proud to hear all those messages from this pulpit and you should mobilize. Depending on the company you keep, you may find yourself with Jews leaning this way or that way, questioning the loyalties of Jews who think otherwise. Be the upstander, be the person who stops that conversation mid-sentence to say: "You may disagree with their views. I may disagree with their views, but their views are rooted in Jewish sources and a love for the Jewish people." And should you be told that you need to choose between the particular and universal – or, more likely, if you are just so exhausted and confused that you are tempted to throw up your hands because it is just too complicated to take a stand, fight that urge!

"If not now – then when?" Now is the time to stand up for justice. "If not now – then when?" Now is the time to stand up to antisemitism. Now is the time to take up Israel's cause. Now is the time to address the climate crisis. If we, in this room – blessed as we are with the political, social, and philanthropic wherewithal to move the needle on the urgent issues of the hour, representing, more or less, the sane center, the moral ballast of the American Jewish community – if we abdicate our role in the unfolding dramas of our time, then we will have failed not only our forebears, failed not only the calling of the hour, but we will have failed our children and grandchildren. "If not now, then when?" If you ever wondered what you would have done if you were alive at the time of the civil rights movement, at the time of the Six-Day War, in 1942, in 1882, now is the time to find out. If there is one message of these holidays, it is that we have a limited amount of time to make a difference in this world. Now is the time to lead by way of example.

Ours is not the first era in which Jews have openly wrestled to define Jewish self-interest. Ours is not the first hour that the Jewish commitment to our people and the Jewish commitment to our shared humanity must be negotiated. This is not the first Rosh Hashanah that Jews have been called upon to take a stand on the issues of the day.

So let us resolve to do what must be done. To stand up for our beliefs, wrestle with them openly and honestly and in respectful dialogue with those who differ. Let us debate ideas and not allegiance. Let us judge each other generously, as we ourselves would wish to be judged. In the words of Lincoln: "We are not enemies, but friends . . . Though passion may have strained, it must not break our bonds of affection." This is our time to lead, to serve as an example for all of American Jewry, and for all of our country, which once again is in such desperate need of healing.

September 30, 2019
1 Tishrei 5780

Yom Kippur
Do A Mitzvah!

In retrospect . . . those college students . . . they never stood a chance.
    The time was late fall of 1949, and the place was a narrow, dimly lit hallway at 770 Eastern Parkway, the Brooklyn headquarters of the sixth Lubavitcher Rebbe, Rabbi Yosef Yitzhak Schneersohn, by then too frail to go beyond his quarters. Two young men, Shlomo and Zalman, both in their twenties, sat outside their ailing leader's room, singing gentle *niggunim*, wordless Hasidic melodies, which like the young men themselves, were remnants plucked from the ashes of a European Jewry destroyed in the Holocaust just a few years before. (Samuel Heilman, *The Rebbe: The Life and Afterlife of Menachem Mendel Schneerson*, p. 168)
    The Rebbe's door creaked open and the Rebbe's secretary whispered: *Der Rebbe ruft eikh*, "The Rebbe is calling you." The young rabbis were escorted in, directed to sit at the table of the Rebbe, who nodded approvingly as three glasses of schnapps were poured. A blessing was made and the schnapps . . . sipped in silence. Moments passed, and then the Rebbe turned to the young rabbis and uttered seven Yiddish words that would set in motion a revolution, a revolution that continues to this very day: *Keday ir zolt onheybn forn tsu colleges*. "It would be worthwhile for you to start visiting the colleges." America, the Rebbe explained, is a wonderful place – a haven of comfort and security for the Jewish people. But six million Jewish souls had perished in Europe, and now a new generation was

being born in America, a generation whose souls were in danger of being lost, whose souls must be saved. "Go bring them close," instructed the Rebbe as he handed them the bottle of schnapPsalm *Keday ir zolt onheybn forn tsu colleges*. "It would be worthwhile for you to start visiting the colleges."

In the days to follow, the two young men got hold of an old Plymouth and drove in the direction of Boston. They brought with them thirteen pairs of discarded tefillin, a few recordings of Hasidic music on reel-to-reel tapes, and some pamphlets of the Rebbe's teachings. Their first stop was Brandeis University. It was Hanukkah, and they made their way to a holiday party, with jukebox playing, in the Castle – the then student union. The two men entered, and the room turned silent as they set up their accordion, tefillin, and materials. In one corner, the young Shlomo began to sing as he fielded questions from the students. In another corner, Zalman spun Hasidic tales while inviting the students to wrap tefillin with a promise to give a pair of tefillin to anyone able to put them on and take them off three times. Those Brandeis students . . . they didn't know what hit them; they never stood a chance. Those two men were not just any men. Shlomo was Rabbi Shlomo Carlebach – the man who would over the course of his lifetime, notwithstanding his personal failings, revolutionize the canon of American Jewish music. Zalman, his friend, was Rabbi Zalman Schachter (later Schachter-Shalomi) – the founder of the Jewish Renewal movement, one of the most creative Jewish minds of the twentieth century. The students hung onto the rabbis' every word and sang every melody. By dawn, thirteen pairs of tefillin had been handed out, thirteen Jewish lives transformed by the performance of a *mitzvah*. A Hanukkah – which means rededication – to remember. American Judaism would never be the same. (Aryae Coopersmith, *Holy Beggars: A Journey from Haight Street to Jerusalem*)

Soon after that historic Hanukkah, the sixth Lubavitcher Rebbe passed. His charge to Shlomo and Zalman was one of his last directives to his students. A year later, on the occasion of his first yahrzeit, Menachem Mendel Schneersohn was appointed the seventh Lubavitcher Rebbe, and at the *farbrengen*, the festive gathering, marking the beginning of his leadership, he gave voice to the vision and mission going forward. In Schneerson's words: "One must go to a place where nothing is known of Godliness, nothing is known of Judaism, nothing is even known of the Hebrew alphabet, and while there, put one's own self aside and ensure that the other calls out to God!" (Joseph Telushkin, *Rebbe: The Life and Teachings of Menachem M. Schneerson, The Most Influential Rabbi in Modern History*) In the years ahead, the Rebbe would dispatch emissaries across the country and globe, on street corners, mitzvah mobiles, and otherwise – campaigns (*mivtzaot*) encouraging tefillin, Shabbat candles, *kashrut*, Torah study, *tzedakah, mezuzah, mikveh*, among other *mitzvot*. What was for Rabbis Carlebach and Shachter an impromptu act of outreach would become, in the hands of Schneerson, a worldwide campaign.

This fall marks seventy years since that fateful evening of outreach and twenty-five years since the death of the Lubavitcher Rebbe. It would be understandable if, in reviewing American Jewish life of the last seventy years, one were to overlook the profound achievements of Chabad. In the decades since the Shoah, our people, thank God, have had our share of success stories, including synagogues like our own, the Hillel movement, Jewish camping, Birthright trips, Holocaust memorials, Jewish studies departments, and the greatest success of all – the State of Israel. Chabad is perhaps the most unexpected player in the landscape of American Jewish life. From a cultural curiosity in the nineteen forties and fifties, Chabad has blossomed into a vast, dynamic, and ever-growing network. With over three hundred Chabad Houses on campus and five thousand *sheluchim*, emissary families, Chabad can boast a foothold in all fifty states, not to mention a formidable online presence. Simply put, the last seventy years of American Jewish history could not be written without mention of Chabad's manifold achievements.

And at the core of it all, the spark that got it all going is one word – *mitzvah*. An all hands-on-deck, non-judgment pass, full court press, to have as many Jews as possible perform as many *mitzvot* as possible. Chabad's mitzvah campaigns are not, by any stretch, the only tactic of the last seven decades to revitalize Jewish life. Ultra-Orthodox communities have built enclaves isolated from the corrupting influences of the secular world. Progressive communities have assimilated elements of the non-Jewish world into Jewish practice. Zionists have walked away from America altogether, believing only Israel can guarantee the Jewish future. Chabad functions in the same landscape; they have just responded with a different tactic. The Rebbe routinely referred to the United States as a *malkhut shel ḥesed*, a government of kindness. He understood the blessings of our country better than anyone. But what he also understood was that such blessings came with a challenge, the challenge of how American Jews could differentiate themselves within such hospitable surroundings. Which meant that for the Rebbe, *mitzvot* were the key – the performance of a *mitzvah*, a distinctly Jewish act – tefillin, Shabbat candles, making challah, or otherwise. That is the key, the secret sauce by which the assimilated American Jew would find a way back into *yiddishkeit*.

Before I say another word, lest you be wondering, I am not outing myself today as a Chabadnik, and Park Avenue Synagogue is not turning into a Chabad House. But with regard to the performance of *mitzvot* – distinct and differentiated Jewish deeds – on that front there is no daylight between me and my Chabad friends. Schneerson was right about the direction of American Jewry in ways that even he didn't imagine possible. We live with freedoms the likes of which prior generations could only have dreamt about. An upwardly mobile community that enjoys hard-earned political, social, and economic blessings. An American Jewry who live in unprecedented comfort with regard to antisemitism. An American Jewry who, by dint of the efforts of our brothers and sisters across the ocean, are living in the era of the longest period of Jewish self-sovereignty in 2000 years. It's not that we don't have problems – of course we do – but the problems American Jews face are, by and large, the high-class kind – derived from the blessing of having options, of having power and privilege, of being accepted and loved by our non-Jewish neighbors. If I had to choose the problems of any Jewish generation throughout history, hands down I would choose ours any day of the week.

But what is good for Jews is not always good for Judaism.

The philosopher Ernst Renan once explained that a people is sustained by the shared memory of a past and the willingness to continue that heritage as a common possession. The unintended consequence of the blessings enjoyed by American Jews, of our acceptance by this *malkhut shel ḥesed*, is that our collective memories, our common bonds and shared language, have withered. The crisis, however, runs deeper. The fact of our freedom, after all, is not new – Schneerson understood it well seventy years ago. What is new, what our generation must contend with that past generations never did, is the fraying of our unspoken safety net, the three things that rightly or wrongly American Jews could always count on to keep us together, but can do so no longer: 1) The Shoah, 2) Israel, 3) Antisemitism.

First, the Shoah. When I went to Hebrew school, I was taught about the 614th commandment – that in addition to the 613 commandments, after the Holocaust there is an additional commandment – to remain Jewish lest we provide Hitler a posthumous victory. But more important than what was being taught, was who was teaching: Hebrew School teachers with concentration camp numbers tattooed on their arms. Seventy years later, our commitment to the memory of those murdered in the Shoah remains resolute and eternal. But for Jewish educators, it is neither practical, nor for that matter, conscionable to leverage the horrors of the Shoah to prompt positive Jewish identification in the next generation. The Shoah can no longer be counted on to inspire individual or collective Jewish identity.

Second, Israel. For seventy years, Israel has been the centripetal force keeping American Jews together. In '67, '73, Entebbe, Osirak, in triumph and tragedy, Israel has brought us close. But you and I both know that for the coming generation that is no longer the case. Israel alienates as many American Jews as it engages. Ours is an era where our opinions regarding Israel divide as much as they unite. And as for the extraordinary success of Birthright, Honeymoon Israel, Onward Israel, and all the other Israel programs that you should support and send your children and grandchildren on, none of them answer that question of how and why to live an engaged Jewish life once you return from Israel to America. Israel can no longer be counted on to inspire individual or collective Jewish identity.

Third, Antisemitism. Notwithstanding the hatreds about which I spoke on Rosh Hashanah, American Jewry is living in an unprecedented era of social tolerance. Say what you will, the state-sponsored antisemitism of other times and other places is simply not the lived experience of American Jewry. A blessing to be sure, but also a challenge. To paraphrase the provocative comment of the late Rabbi Arthur Hertzberg: The only thing worse for a Jew than antisemitism is no antisemitism. Why? Because then the onus for a Jew to be a Jew is on nobody but themselves. Besides, what sort of Judaism is it, if it is reliant on the hatreds of others in order to survive? Antisemitism can no longer be counted on to inspire individual or collective Jewish identity.

The Shoah, Israel, and antisemitism. These were the three forces, the threefold mystic cord that we could always count on. Three constants that even Schneerson could fall back on to keep the Jewish people together. Three constants that are constant no longer.

Which is why we need *mitzvot*. *Mitzvot* – the commitments and commandments – the sparks that can inspire individual and collective Jewish identity. The proud performance of Jewish deeds that are not contingent on the Shoah, that have nothing to do with how we feel about Israel, and that exist independently of antisemitism. Let me be clear: I am not talking about being kind, about a nebulous plea to live according to some inchoate set of Jewish values. I am talking about *kashrut*, about prayer, about Torah study, about coming to shul, about tzedakah and yes – tefillin and Shabbat candles, too. I am talking about the Jewish obligation and opportunity to perform distinctly Jewish acts on your own and in the company of other Jews. I am talking about *mitzvot*.

There, I finally said it. It's been more than a decade, and I am saying the very thing a rabbi is supposed to say: I am asking you to do *mitzvot*. You know the old story about the young rabbi who arrives at his new congregation fresh from rabbinical school. He consults with the chairman on ideas for his first sermon. He wants to talk about

Israel; the chairman counsels against it, explaining that the community is divided on Israel. The young rabbi pivots and says that he will speak about Jewish business ethics; the chairman again counsels otherwise, lest the rabbi unknowingly offend a congregant. Yet again the young rabbi pivots, to the well-worn theme of *lashon hara*, gossip; and the chairman cautions the rabbi that that theme too would upset his chattier congregants. Exasperated, the young rabbi pleads: "I can't talk about Israel, I can't talk about ethics, I can't talk about gossip; what do you want me to talk about?" To which the chairman replies: "Judaism! Why not just talk about Judaism?"

The story is supposed to be a joke, only this time it is no joke, or at least the joke is on us. Over the years I have spoken to you about Israel, I have spoken to you about ethics, I have spoken to you about gossip. Today, I am talking about the thing I have avoided all these years: Judaism. The Jewish obligation and opportunity to perform distinctly Jewish acts on your own and in the company of other Jews. *Mitzvot*. The shared language that has kept our people together through ages. The Proustian madeleines, the triggers to memory that have kept our people together – across continents and through the generations – the sparks that have ignited the Jewish soul throughout the ages.

For the spiritually minded, *mitzvot* are the gestures that we make, the rituals we do to express our vertical relationship to the divine. The relationships in my life that mean the most to me – my wife, my parents, my children, defy the limitations of words. So I express those relationships in deeds, in actions – daily, weekly, and seasonally – that reflect the covenantal bonds that we share. It is simply beyond my ability to give voice to the joy of being alive and, when faced with it, the unspeakable sorrow that comes with the limits of my humanity. I have no words – so I turn to *mitzvot*. *Mitzvot* are what make the mundane sacred, the agonizing tolerable, and the presence of God palpable when I need it most and feel it least. It was Louis Finkelstein, the late chancellor of JTS, who reflected: "When I pray, I speak to God; when I study Torah, God speaks to me." When I light Shabbat candles, when I put on tefillin every day, when I refrain from eating from one side of the menu in favor of the other; I am – to use Heschel's language – taking a leap of action. I am giving expression to a vertical relationship to a God in heaven who exists well beyond the limitations of speech. *Mitzvot* are the sacred vocabulary that a Jew draws upon to express his or her relationship with the divine.

I know, for many of us, theology is not enough; Or more precisely, it is too much – a leap of faith too far. You don't subscribe, you say, to a commanding God, to outdated notions of reward and punishment. Instead, I encourage you to think of *mitzvot* not in the vertical, as a connection to a God above, but in the horizontal, a connection to your fellow Jew. The great twentieth-century thinker Rabbi Mordecai Kaplan spoke of *mitzvot* as folkways – the shared customs that constitute the Jewish civilization. Every community has its folkways, the behaviors and regimens – daily, seasonal, and otherwise – that make a community a community and each one of us a part of that community. Folkways that mark the passage of time and personal transformations, that connect us to a past that long precedes us and a future well beyond the horizon of our brief years. The architecture by which we build a conscious community. Why are we here in shul today? Two million American Jews, according to the Pew study, are in synagogue, fasting and praying prayers – some of which we understand, a whole bunch we probably don't. Why? Our very presence here today signals that we intuitively understand the power of *mitzvot* as folkways. My only question, and I am getting ahead of myself, is whether we can extend that intuition beyond this one day.

There are all sorts of reasons to observe *mitzvot*, probably as many reasons as there are *mitzvot*, not the least of which is, speaking personally, that I quite enjoy them. Today I would ask you to consider the most basic reason of all: *mitzvot* as positive acts of Jewish self-identification. For many years, Jews have lived according to Yehuda Leib Gordon's dictum of being "a Jew in the home and a man on the street" – to keep the fact of our Jewish identity hidden from public eye. As American Jews our lives are akin to story of the man on the subway reading the paper, sitting across from a lady, who staring at him intently, eventually asks: "Excuse me sir? Are you Jewish?" The man politely replies: "No." Moments pass, and the woman again inquires: "I am sorry to bother you, but are you sure you are not Jewish?" Again, the man politely, but this time firmly, replies: No, he is not Jewish. The lady can't help herself: "Sir, I have to ask . . . Are you absolutely, positively sure you are not Jewish?" At which point the man slaps down his paper, looks up exasperatedly, and blurts out: "You know what, lady, you are right – you got me – I am Jewish!" To which the lady replies: "Funny, because you don't look Jewish."

The positive and open expression of your Jewish self: that is the argument for a *mitzvah*. Think about the choreography; I imagine most everyone in the room has been invited to the dance at least once. First, the question: "Excuse me, are you Jewish?" And then, the follow-up. If you are a man: "Would you like to put on tefillin?" Or, if you are a woman: "Would you like to learn how to light Shabbos candles?" The question is not an "ask." It is an offer, an invitation, perhaps even a challenge. Would you, by way of performing this distinctly Jewish act, this *mitzvah*, please self-identify as a Jew? Performing a *mitzvah* is a proud transformation of the universal self into a Jewish self, making manifest one's particular identity by way of the decision of what to eat, how to structure one's time, and how to present oneself to the world. Why should you observe *mitzvot*? Because doing so is the means by which you express pride in who you are and in where you came from and your hope that those who come after you will feel and do the same. There is no greater act of Jewish self-assertion, empowerment, and hope than the performance of a *mitzvah*. To do a *mitzvah* is to take agency for your spiritual life.

I am not a Chabadnik for all sorts of reasons. To name but a few: I have a more expansive definition of mitzvah than they do. I have a more inclusive and egalitarian definition of the Jewish people than they do. And I have a far more progressive notion of how Jewish law develops than they do. But I am your rabbi, so let's put it out there: Can this year be the year you take on *mitzvot* in your life? I don't need them all, I am an incrementalist. I believe that one *mitzvah* leads to another. Just don't tell me that ritual is not your thing or that you can't make the time. Our lives are filled with rituals: timebound, dietary, and seasonal.

We go to Soul Cycle, we go to yoga, we eat GG crackers for God's sake! We carve out time for marathons, we shlep to the new workout in SoHo, and we freeze on the sidelines of our children's club sports in God knows where. We can prioritize just fine – when we deem something to be a priority! American Jews are full of *mitzvot*, just not the Jewish ones. I want you to take on the Jewish ones! I want you to take agency for your spiritual life. *Mitzvot* are not the sole domain of the Orthodox – they belong to all of us! Let's give the Jewish world something to talk about – a Conservative synagogue proudly and passionately pursuing *mitzvot*. The great twentieth-century Jewish thinker Franz Rosenzweig, when asked whether he put on tefillin, replied "Not yet." Let this year be the year. Here in this room, right now, take the time to reflect, reflect with your family: how can you move from "not my thing," to "not yet," to "why not, let's see what happens." "Taste and see," teaches the psalmist. (Psalm 34:9) Be open to performing one holy deed and see what happens next. As Maimonides taught, all it takes is one deed to tip the balance in one direction or the other. *(Laws of Repentance 3: 4)*

And let this synagogue, my colleagues and I, guide you in your efforts. The theme of our fall programming, as announced by our chairman and as outlined in the brochure on your seats, is "rededication." Yes – our physical building will be rededicated in time for Hanukkah. But today it is the spiritual architecture of your year ahead that is my concern and that should be yours. If you don't know how to put on tefillin, to put up a mezuzah, to open up a prayer book, to study a Jewish text, to make your home kosher – we are here for you. My colleagues and I would love to spend time with you teaching you how to prepare a shabbat table, light shabbat candles, and say kiddush. Come to think of it, that is actually what you hired us to do! The Rebbe himself was once asked: "What is a rabbi good for?" He replied: "The Earth contains all kinds of treasures, you just have to know where to dig. If you do not, you will come up not with diamonds, but rocks and mud. That's why you need a geologist – to tell you how and where to dig. *What is a rabbi good for?* A rabbi is a geologist of the soul. But a rabbi can only show you where to dig. The actual digging . . . you must do yourself . . ." (Z. Schachter Shalomi, *The Geologist to the Soul: Talks on Rebbe-craft and Spiritual Leadership*) How amazing would it be if, when we dedicate our building in December, when we light that Hanukkah menorah with candles representing the spectrum of Jewish deeds, seventy years after that Hanukkah on the Brandeis campus, you are able to reflect on your own Jewish life, dedicated and rededicated to proud Jewish living.

The closest Park Avenue Synagogue ever came to becoming a Chabad House was in 1966 when, under the leadership of one of my predecessors, Rabbi Judah Nadich of blessed memory, Rabbi Shlomo Carlebach was invited to teach and sing in the synagogue for an evening. By way of the Shapiro Audio Archive on our website, I listened to a recording of that evening. I invite you to do the same after *yontif*.

It was a moving program, a taste of Hasidus here on the Upper East Side, an evening that concluded with Rabbi Carlebach singing *Am Yisroel Chai*, "The people of Israel live." Before concluding, he spoke, and I would like to share with you what he said. He said:

> "You know, if I put a piece of chicken on the table, you have to chew it yourself. I can only put it on the table; you gotta work yourself. The story is told of two Hasidim from two different *hevres*, sects, who met up. One says to the other: 'Tell me, great rabbi, what is the most important thing to you?' The other says: 'The most important thing is whatever I am doing at that very moment.'"

And Reb Shlomo concluded: "That is the most important thing to him. That means he is ready. He is ready to give his life to every act he is doing."

Friends, if there is a message of Yom Kippur, it is that every act – every *mitzvah* – matters. We need to take agency for our spiritual lives; living intentionally, proudly and passionately as Jews. The fallbacks of the last seventy years no longer suffice. In order for *Am Yisrael Chai*, for the people of Israel to live, we must draw on the tools that date back to the very origins of our people – *mitzvot*. Me, I can only put the chicken on the table – it is your job to chew. One bite at a time, one *mitzvah* at a time. Let this year be the year for your Jewish spark to shine forth brightly for all the world to see.

October 8, 2019
9 Tishrei 5780

Yom Kippur Yizkor
The Parochet

This summer marked the seventieth anniversary of the reinterment of Theodor Herzl in Israel. Herzl, the founder of political Zionism, died in 1904 at the age of forty-four. Though he died in Vienna, Herzl made clear in his last will and testament his wish to be buried in the Jewish homeland – a dream to most but in Herzl's mind, a foregone conclusion. When the State of Israel was founded in 1948, Israel's first Prime Minister, David Ben-Gurion, saw to it that the physical remains of its founding ideologue – Herzl – would be brought home. Ben-Gurion's words that August day of 1949 framed the import of the moment for Israelis and for us today at this moment of Yizkor. "Only two people," noted Ben-Gurion, "have had the privilege of having their remains brought to Israel by their liberated nation. Joseph from Egypt and Herzl from Vienna." (Doron Bar, *Landscape and Ideology: Reinterment of Renowned Jews in the Land of Israel (1904–1967)*, p. 36) Ben-Gurion understood that this moment was not just about physical retrieval, but spiritual as well: the honoring of the past, the creation of collective conscience, and a meditation on how the values of our forebears inform our own lives. Just as Joseph commanded his kin, just as Herzl instructed his descendants, today, here in this room, we fulfill the *mitzvah*, the obligation, of retrieving the memories of those individuals without whom we would not be here – neither individually nor as a community.

Today, I want to share with you another aspect of the Herzl story – not about Herzl's final resting place, but about the cloth, the funeral pall, the *parochet*, that covered Herzl's casket on August 17, 1949.

In the decades immediately following Herzl's passing, there was no way anyone could act on Herzl's request to be buried in the Jewish homeland. In 1935, the Zionist movement saw a window of opportunity and, at the 19th Zionist Congress in Lucerne, Switzerland, agreed to move Herzl's remains to British-controlled Palestine. A Viennese artist, Arthur Weisz, was commissioned to design the *parochet* for the occasion. It was a gorgeous achievement: two meters long, one-and-a-half meters wide, with two biblical verses and the final passage of Herzl's famous book *Der Judenstaat* embroidered on it. A blue and white motif, gold stitching, the image of a lion inside a star of David, and seven gold stars reminiscent of Herzl's original proposal for the flag of the imagined Jewish state. That window of opportunity, however, did not last. The situation of European Jewry grew precarious, priorities shifted, and the plans to reinter Herzl were postponed indefinitely. In 1939, Arthur Weisz's *parochet* did make it to Mandatory Palestine, to be stored in the JNF building in Tel Aviv. Weisz, however, did not. He was murdered in 1942 in Auschwitz. His wife and children survived the war hidden in France, saved by righteous gentiles.

One can only imagine the emotions that August day in 1949 when Herzl was reinterred in Jerusalem. "If you will it, it is no dream" – Herzl's last will and testament fulfilled by burial in the sovereign state of Israel. Curiously, at the conclusion of the ceremony, the *parochet*, which was meant to go on display in the "Herzl Room" at the JNF building, was lost. In the next decades, though good will efforts were made and conspiracy theories abounded, the *parochet*, alas, was never found.

Arthur's son Yitzhak was only three when separated from his father. He grew up in France, trained as an endodontist, met his wife Isabelle, and made *aliyah* to Israel in the early 1970s, going on to raise three children and then twelve grandchildren. Yitzhak has no recollection of his father, his only knowledge of him constructed by way of his late mother's stories. He knew that his father had been an artist. There are *haggadot* and woodcuts with his signature, but no evidence of a link to Herzl. His mother had once made mention of something, but Yitzhak Weisz dismissed it. As far as he knew, the *parochet* was created in 1949 in Israel for the reinterment service, and his father Arthur had been murdered in 1942.

And that is where things stood until one day in 1998 when Yitzhak and Isabelle took a vacation to Kibbutz Hagoshrim in the Upper Galilee. Isabelle decided to take a dip in the pool, and Yitzhak, lying in the sun on his chaise lounge, woke from his nap and picked up the book Isabelle had been reading. The book was *Altneuland*, Herzl's utopian fictional romance. Yitzhak read it cover to cover and, to Isabelle's astonishment, read it over and over again. Something about the book prompted Yitzhak to reconsider the story of Herzl that he – and all Jewish kids – had been taught growing up. His intrigue became an obsession and over the next seven years, he spent every moment that he was not in his clinic deep in the Zionist archives writing a new assessment of Herzl and his relevancy for Israel today. Dedicated, appropriately, to Weisz's now late wife Isabelle, it was published in 2005 in French and has just been translated into English: *Theodor Herzl: A New Reading*, available on Kindle for a modest $7.00. In all those years, Yitzhak had no idea of the connection between his late father and Herzl. The thought never crossed his mind.

Which is where things stood until December 14, 2005 – a day that Yitzhak shares as one of the most important days of his life. Having spent years in the Zionist archives researching Herzl, and having submitted his book for publication, one morning Yitzhak found himself with a few spare minutes before his day at the clinic began. He wandered into a Jerusalem bookstore where the front page of *Haaretz* from August 17, 1949 was on display, complete with a picture of the reinterment ceremony, with Herzl's casket center stage, draped in the *parochet*. What caught Yitzhak's attention was not the picture – an iconic image that every Israeli has seen many times. What stopped him in his tracks was the journalistic footnote that the *parochet* had been made not in Israel in 1949, but in Vienna in 1936. Yitzhak's mother had long since passed, but he remembered her offhand comment, and he dove back into the Zionist Archives to examine all the files pertaining to Herzl's reinterment. It was there that he discovered that it was his father, Arthur Weisz, who had designed that *parochet* together with Oskar Strand. (Central Zionist Archives S/10/426) Just imagine how Yitzhak felt at that moment of discovery. Not just that his father, murdered in Auschwitz, was, as it were, a posthumous participant in the Zionist narrative; but that Yitzhak had spent seven years researching the very topic that connected him to the father he never knew. Yitzhak got involved in the anniversary planning, and a replica of the lost *parochet* was made. One can only imagine how Yitzhak felt this past summer, when the replica of his father's original *parochet* was presented at the ceremony on Mount Herzl with Prime Minister Netanyahu and President Rivlin present. It was an expression of *kibud av*, honoring one's father – in the words of the son a reminder to all, "that one of those six million murdered in the Holocaust was a Jew named Arthur Weisz."

And that is where things stood until the day after the ceremony. Some time ago, it was decided that the JNF warehouse buildings in Tel Aviv would be sold and turned into a boutique hotel. Which meant that this summer was when everything had to be cleared out of the building. You will never guess what they found on the day *after* the seventieth anniversary ceremony! There it was: folded-up under a cupboard, a little gray, untouched for seventy years – the missing *parochet* of Arthur Weisz. At that point, I decided to stop imagining and start asking. I called Dr. Yitzhak Weisz, now eighty-one, still a practicing endodontist. Dr. Weisz shared with me the indescribable feeling that came with seeing his father's original handiwork, touching the very cloth that his father had touched, brushing it against his cheek . . . in his words: "to feel the fingerprints of his father," the man he never knew, as close to him at that moment as he had ever been – in life or in death.

In case you are wondering, I did ask Dr. Weisz about the plans for the *parochet* now that it has been found. It is sitting in the town of Modiin; the JNF (Jewish National Fund) and WZO (World Zionist Organization) are in the midst of legal proceedings over which Zionist organization it belongs to. The story, it would seem, continues.

Friends, ours is the moment of Yizkor. Now is the time to enter the cupboards, the warehouses of memory. Some of the loved ones we recall were intimates, people with whom we journeyed through the chapters of life – brothers and sisters, spouses, children, parents, and friends. Some, we only knew from a distance, the stories of their lives relayed to us by others. The project of Yizkor, of remembering, is nevertheless one and the same for us all. We hold the memories close, as close as a cloth brushing against our cheek, and we look to connect. We ask how the lives of our loved ones inform our own. What were their values? What were their triumphs? What were their setbacks? What can we learn from them? How can we honor them in our own lives? How shall we fulfill the unfinished legacies they bequeathed to us? We have been diminished by their passing, and our loss can overwhelm, but memories . . . can still teach.

One final thought, one last image, one last loose end. Aside from the passage from Herzl's *Der Judenstaat*, what were those two biblical verses that Arthur Weisz chose to embroider on his *parochet* in 1936? The first, from the book of Ezekiel, speaks to Weisz's commission of 1936: "Behold, I will open your graves and cause you to come out of your graves, O My People; and I will bring you into the Land of Israel." (Ezekiel 37:12) The second, more familiar to us, is from the book of Psalms: "Those who sow in tears shall reap in joy." (126:5) Always, and especially at this Yizkor hour, we know that the tears of sorrow flow freely. But as Yitzhak Weisz came to discover, from those tears of sorrow can come comfort, redemption, and sometimes even joy. May that be our blessing this Yizkor. May the tears we shed today bring with them the gift of memory, the gift of comfort, and one day – in the unknown future – the promise of joy.

October 9, 2019
10 Tishrei 5780

Sukkot, Day 1
Builders

In the history of collaborative friendships – Sherlock Holmes and Watson, Tina Fey and Amy Poehler, Bruce Springsteen and Clarence Clemons – in the category of Modern Jewish Thought, first among equals is the friendship between Martin Buber and Franz Rosenzweig. Despite a nearly nine-year gap in age, despite the fact that Rosenzweig's spiritual trajectory was a passage from a secular youth into tradition, while Buber's was a journey away from the traditionalism of his youth, for a handful of years the intellectual, institutional, and spiritual collaboration of these two intellectual giants set the contours of the Jewish conversation in pre-war Germany and arguably for decades to come. As told by my doctoral advisor, Paul Mendes-Flohr, in his fabulous new biography of Buber, the two men first met when Rosenzweig paid Buber a brief visit at his Berlin residence in 1914. In the years ahead the two would review each other's writings and participate in each other's publications. Buber would lecture to hundreds at Rosenzweig's Frankfurt Lehrhaus – the site of an interwar renaissance of German-Jewish learning. Their shared intellectual and spiritual bond seeded perhaps their boldest and most tragic shared venture: a translation of the Hebrew Bible into German, reflecting their shared desire to make the Torah come alive to a non-Hebrew reading German Jewry. They worked on it together, even as Rosenzweig was stricken with ALS, leading to his death in 1929. Buber, who emigrated to Palestine in 1938, ultimately completed the translation in 1961, by which time the German Jewry whom they had sought to bring close to tradition no longer existed. Buber dedicated the translation to Rosenzweig

– a small gesture reflecting the immeasurable bond of intellectual and spiritual friendship the two had shared. (Mendes-Flohr, *Martin Buber: A Life of Faith and Dissent*)

This morning, I would like to focus on one of the most famous exchanges between the two men, which takes off from one of the most famous exchanges regarding today's festival of Sukkot. The primary *mitzvah* of our festival is clearly stated in today's Torah reading: "You shall dwell in *sukkot*, booths, seven days . . . that your generations know that I made the children of Israel dwell in *sukkot*, when I brought them out of the land of Egypt: I am the Lord your God." (Leviticus 23:42–43) At first blush, the verse appears rather straightforward. Just as the children of Israel dwelt in booths in their wilderness wanderings, so we are commanded to do so through the generations. Rabbi Akiva states in the Talmud that it is a commandment to be understood literally: Build *sukkot*. Rabbi Eliezer, however, understands the verse to refer not to a physical structure, but a spiritual one – *ananei kavod*, clouds of glory. (Babylonian Talmud: Sukkah 11b) To Rabbi Eliezer, the language of *sukkot* is just a metaphor: Not only is God's presence not contingent on a *sukkah*, but the very notion that one would rely on the structure of a *sukkah* in order to sense God's presence is actually contrary to how God's presence is experienced. The debate is not just between Rabbi Eliezer and Akiva; it continues through the ages. The eleventh-century commentator Rashi understands the verse as Rabbi Eliezer did – to refer to clouds of glory. Rashbam, Rashi's grandson, disagrees with Rabbi Eliezer and with his own grandfather, explaining that *sukkot* are the very vehicles by which we achieve a sense of the divine. So many rabbis, over such an expanse of time, disagreeing over one verse! One senses that more than a matter of lexical interpretation is at stake. Rather, at stake is a matter of substantive theological difference. How is God's presence to be experienced? Must one build a structure in order to experience God's presence; or, more provocatively, is the very act of building a sukkah actually an impediment to that theological goal?

This debate about *sukkot* – from Eliezer and Akiva through Rashi and Rashbam – continues with Buber and Rosenzweig. To the best of my knowledge, Buber and Rosenzweig never actually debated *sukkot*, but they did debate the architecture by which our people are meant to experience God's presence. They did this in a series of letters that I will be teaching tomorrow night in the sukkah. (I invite you to come to the evening session in preparation for the visit of Dr. Paul Mendes-Flohr on October 24, when he will discuss his new book on Buber with our community.)

Our story begins in Vienna in 1918 with a lecture that Buber delivered to a Zionist youth group called "*Ḥerut* [Freedom]: On Youth and Religion." Seeking to prompt a renaissance in Jewish life, Buber tried to give voice to the three primary sources of Jewish religiosity. *torato*, *amo*, and *atzmo*. That is, it is by way of connection to text (*torato*), to one's people (*amo*) and to one's self (*atzmo*) that a Jew expresses his or her own faith. Buber wrote at length on all three sources of connection, and while now is not the time to go into detail about each one, he held that it is by way of these three pathways – our literature, our nationhood, and our individual spiritual striving – that authentic Jewish religious life is to be found. Interestingly, in Buber's mind these spiritual forces were not distributed equally throughout Jewish history. They were present in the Biblical narratives; they were present in the time of the prophets; they were the driving elements in the rise of Hasidism. They were not present, however – and this is the rub – in the time of rabbinic literature – which for Buber would always remain just "hairsplitting casuistry," the exilic edifice of legislation that impeded, rather than enabled, authentic spiritual behavior. For Buber, Jewish renewal required one to eschew doctrinal orthodoxy in order to access the primal forces of the Jewish people. Simply put: God's presence is best felt without the *sukkah* of Jewish law.

In response, Rosenzweig penned an open letter to his friend entitled "The Builders." The letter's title is a play on a famous midrashic passage: Commenting on the verse "And all thy children (*banayikh*) shall be taught of Lord . . ." (Isaiah 54:13), the midrash states: "Do not read *banayikh*, your children, but *bonayikh*, your builders." In other words, for Rosenzweig, it is the very act of fulfilling the law by which we not only build the sacred architecture, the *sukkah*, to house God's presence, but we also set our children on the path toward perpetuating Israel's covenant with God. In language both beautiful and biting, Rosenzweig takes Buber to task for his dismissive approach to Jewish law. He writes:

> Is it really Jewish law with which you try to come to terms? ... Is that really Jewish law, the law of millennia, studied and lived, analyzed and rhapsodized, the law of everyday and the day of death, petty and yet sublime, sober and yet woven in legend; a law which knows both the fire of the sabbath candle and that of the martyr's stake ... ? *(Franz Rosenzweig: His Life and Thought.* Ed. N. Glatzer, pp. 237-238)

For Rosenzweig, the performance of a *mitzvah* is the ultimate expression of Jewish religiosity: a Jew's response to divine love. A commandment from God is a form of divine address to which a Jew can respond by way of inner power. Even if, as Rosenzweig concedes possible, the law itself is not divine, it is in the performance of a commandment that a Jew comes closest to accessing the divine will. Surely Buber, who well understood the sacred potentiality of Jewish study, of connection to one's people and to one's self, could relate to the power of performing a *mitzvah*, a commandment.

But Buber, as he would make clear in his response to Rosenzweig, could not. Buber would only ever see *halakhah*, Jewish law, as *Gesetz* – the German word for law –but never *Gebote* – an expression of the divine will. In Buber's estimation, commandments are, by definition, coercive in nature, and thus to observe them is somehow to stifle the human spirit. Even worse, to observe Jewish law merely because it was passed on to you by a prior generation is akin to some sort of crude ancestor worship. Having come from a traditional background, Buber did not take lightly his rejection of Jewish law. On the eve of Yom Kippur in 1922, he confessed to Rosenzweig that his decision not to fast on Yom Kippur was far more difficult for him than had he decided to fast. The absence of Jewish ritual and prayer from his life had left a void – a void that could not be filled with anything else. Buber nevertheless remained resolute in his conviction that God's presence could not be felt by way of the structure, the *sukkah*, of Jewish law. The letters between Buber and Rosenzweig continued back and forth – the issue never resolved. For Rosenzweig, it was ritual observance, the rhythms of Jewish prayer, the shared sacred calendar that are the cherished acts by which a Jew gives expression to his or her covenantal relationship to God. For Buber, it was these very acts that precluded the authentic striving of the religious soul.

I can think of no better time than this festival of Sukkot to meditate on their famous debate. Sukkot directs us to build shelters according to certain specifications, shelters worthy of housing God's presence. But more than that, Sukkot is the festival of ritual par excellence. We say particular prayers, we take a lulav and etrog into our hands, we walk in circles around the sanctuary singing *hoshanot* reenacting the ancient temple ritual. We do all sorts of things – things called *mitzvot*, commandments. For some, these *mitzvot* are the very keys toward living an elevated, sacred, and holy existence; for others, *mitzvot* are the very things that alienate us from our faith and maybe even ourselves. The debate, after all, did not end with the passing of these two giants of twentieth-century thought. It is a debate that continues to be played out in yoga studios, Soul Cycle classes, synagogue pews, and wherever Jews are to be found. How shall we best access God's presence? How can the riches of the Jewish tradition facilitate the contemporary spiritual quest? Buber and Rosenzweig, Akiva and Eliezer, Rashi and Rashbam all had a point. Woe unto the generation that does not acknowledge both sides of the debate.

Which is, I suppose, the point: the point of the debate and the point of our holiday. If nothing else, Sukkot reminds us of our obligation to be hospitable, to welcome people into our sukkah, around our tables, and into our lives – even those voices, perhaps especially those voices, with whom we differ. Rosenzweig, as noted, died tragically young in 1929. At his request, no eulogies were delivered at his funeral. His one request was that Buber read Psalm 73, the psalm containing the verse that Rosenzweig had requested for his gravestone: *va-ani tamid imakh*, I am continually with thee. Did this last request of Rosenzweig's suggest the hope that God would forever be with Rosenzweig? Or maybe Rosenzweig intended it to express a hope that Buber would forever be with him? Who knows? I would like to think a little of both. More importantly, I would like to think it expressed the hope that the questions that these two giants asked would continue with us, their children, *banayikh*, who in keeping the debates of their lives alive in our lifetime will also become *bonayikh*, their builders.

October 14, 2019
15 Tishrei 5780

Hol Ha-moed Sukkot
Jonah's Sukkah

When I was growing up in Los Angeles, there were two things my family always did without fail when we came home from synagogue at the end of Yom Kippur. First, obviously, we broke the fast with lox and bagels. Second, as the final guests left, my father and my brothers and I would begin building our sukkah. Odd as it may have been to roll one holiday directly into the other, at the time I never questioned the tradition. It was something fun to do after a long day in synagogue, and now that I live in the urban jungle of Manhattan, it is something I miss doing with my own children.

It was only years later, in my rabbinical studies, that I discovered that Joseph Karo, the author of the authoritative sixteenth-century code of Jewish law, the *Shulchan Aruch*, had codified this custom long ago. One must make every effort, he writes, to go seamlessly and zealously from one festival to the other, without interruption, by building a sukkah immediately at the conclusion of Yom Kippur. What a sweet feeling to discover years later that the Cosgrove boys were fulfilling not just a demand of my mother, but a commandment from an authority of approximately equal stature – God.

This morning I want to explore this custom from my childhood a bit more. I want to look into the connection between the two holidays, Yom Kippur and Sukkot, and ask what draws this week's festival into dialogue with our recent Day of Atonement. At first blush, the two holidays could not be more different. One is observed in the synagogue for a day, the other in the home for a week. One is about spiritual austerity; the other is the most physical of holidays: building a sukkah and then eating and sleeping in it, circling the Sanctuary, and of course shaking the lulav and etrog. The texts we read on Yom Kippur draw our attention to upstanding moral behavior and the severity of God's judgment. To the degree that Sukkot has a text, it is *Kohelet*, Ecclesiastes, a book that reminds us of the vanity of all human pursuit, the happenstance nature of existence, and the unavoidable fact that one fate awaits us all, rich and poor, righteous and wicked. Sukkot is rooted in history, a re-creation of the Israelites' desert wanderings. Yom Kippur, by contrast, is not tethered to any historical experience. Yes, the two observances sit adjacent one to the other, but aside from that calendrical proximity, is there anything that connects Yom Kippur and Sukkot? Anything that might help explain why we are commanded to build a sukkah immediately after Yom Kippur concludes?

The answer, I believe, can be found in one of the lesser-known scenes of Yom Kippur, from the story of Jonah. If you are not fully familiar with the story, Jonah is the anti-prophet of the Bible. The man who, when God calls on him to tell the people of the city of Nineveh to repent their evil ways, instead flees by ship in the other direction, is thrown overboard, swallowed by a whale, and then spit out onto shore. After drying himself off, Jonah finally does call on Nineveh to repent, and the Ninevites listen to him and are saved from God's wrath. The tale makes for good messaging on Yom Kippur – a day given over to the theme of repentance. But the tale as I just told it, as taught in Hebrew School, misses out on the critical, enigmatic, fourth and final chapter of the book. In that chapter, after God has suspended the divine decree of punishment, after Jonah has saved the city from destruction, Jonah – instead of taking a victory lap on a job well done – slumps into depression, and in a fit of despair, bursts out in frustration at God, saying he was right all along to flee in the ship when he was first called.

It is not altogether clear what is the root of Jonah's anger and toxic malaise. He is embittered at God's inscrutable ways; he is angry that such an evil city has been forgiven so quickly, and he no doubt wonders why, if God already had a plan in mind, he himself needed to be brought in to get involved. In a burst of rage, he cries out to God: "Please Lord, take my life, for I would rather die than live." (4:3) It seems better to Jonah to die than to try to make sense of this whimsical, nonsensical world. And lest you are wondering where I am going with this, you should know that this entire scene – this outburst against God – takes place where? Under a sukkah. A sukkah that Jonah had built east of Nineveh, his planned viewing stand from which to watch Nineveh's destruction, that became the shelter in which he sulked as the city was saved.

So that is the full story of Jonah. And even more important than the content, the "what" of the Jonah story, is the timing, the "when" of our reading it: during the final stretch of Yom Kippur. The very hour when we pray that we will be forgiven like the Ninevites and hopefully be sealed into the Book of Life for the year to come. The thing about Yom Kippur is that while we hope our lives will be filled with health and prosperity in the year to come, none of us actually knows the will or ways of God. All we know is that there are no promises, and no matter how earnestly a person may pray on Yom Kippur, in any given year, on any given day, there will be bad people who will prosper and good people who will suffer. Just yesterday, just days after Yom Kippur, I spent the day at the cemetery with a bereaved synagogue family who lost a brother, a father, a husband, and a grandfather, a man who was, if nothing else, a mensch through and through. We do our best; we pray for forgiveness; and still, this world makes no promises. When you look at it like that, you begin to understand Jonah's anger as he pouts under his sukkah, plunged into despair, exasperated at a God whose ways are so arbitrary, preordained, and yet inexplicable. Can Jonah really be blamed for throwing up his hands and wondering what the point of it all is anyway? Haven't we all felt that way at some time or other?

Which is why, I think, it is precisely at the end of Yom Kippur, with the Jonah story fresh in our minds, that we are commanded to go home and build a sukkah, literally acting out the final scene of Jonah. We know the precarious nature of existence; we know how capricious life can be. If nothing else, the impermanent structure of a sukkah is meant to remind us of the delicate and uncertain nature of our world. Just yesterday, the synagogue had to take down our rooftop sukkah because the high winds made it a hazard not just to anyone inside it, but to anyone on the street below it. One goes home from Yom Kippur to immediately build a sukkah as a physical reminder, should we need one, that in this world there are no promises. We are not so different from Jonah. It would be the most human thing to do to sit in our sukkah sulking like Jonah, despairing at the fragility of our lives.

And that is precisely where the message of Sukkot comes into play. Yom Kippur and Sukkot begin with the same premise: Life is fragile and limited, and God's ways are ultimately unknowable. But their responses are totally different. Yes, Sukkot is all about the happenstance nature of existence, but it demands of us that, given the uncertainty, we rejoice in the blessings we do have. Another name for Sukkot is *Ḥag Ha-asif*, the festival of gathering, an agricultural holiday that reminds us that more than dwelling on what we don't have, we need to celebrate what we do have. We have to thank God for the harvest of our lives. Sukkot is also called *Zman Simḥateinu*, the time of our rejoicing. It is a festival that teaches that awareness of our mortality not only need not throw us into depression, but should prompt us to leverage life for all it is has to offer, to squeeze our loved ones as tight as we can, and never to take for granted the blessings we enjoy.

The book of Ecclesiastes is fully aware of the delicate sukkah-like nature of human existence. But its conclusion, its take-home message, is different from Jonah's. To paraphrase: "Enjoy happiness with the person you love all the fleeting days of life that you have been granted . . . whatever is in your power to do, do with all your might." (9:8-10) It would be understandable to walk through this world like Jonah, with a perpetually wounded sensibility, angry at God, waiting for the other shoe to drop. Sukkot calls on us to fight that urge, this week and year-round: to respond to uncertainty with love, to fragility with strength, and to unwarranted hurt with unjustifiable love. It is this thought that I often share with young couples as they get married under a *ḥuppah*, the wedding canopy that is a conscious reference to a sukkah. What is getting married if not the declaration by two people that in the relatively brief time we have in this world, we choose to spend that time with someone we love who loves us back? Unto itself, a sukkah is morally neutral, a physical reminder of something all of us know already: Life is fragile. The power of Sukkot is in the question it asks of all of us: Given that fragility, will we sit and sulk like Jonah or will we respond with lives filled with meaning, with compassion, with patience, with forgiveness, and with generosity of deed and spirit?

Friends, some of us build *sukkot*. Here in the city I imagine most of us don't; I don't. But all of us live in *sukkot* – this week and every week of our lives. Why do we build *sukkot* immediately after Yom Kippur? To remind us of the choice we have – the choice of how we will live our lives in the next year and years to come. It is not up to God; it is up to each one of us. May we rise to the challenge. In this uncertain and often unfair world, may we see the beauty, may we express the gratitude, and may we fill our days with loving and purposeful deeds that express our highest hopes for ourselves and for this imperfect world in which we are blessed to live.

October 19, 2019
20 Tishrei 5780

B'reishit
#OneYearLater

On this *Shabbat B'reishit*, this sabbath of Creation, our Torah reading describes God placing a fiery ever-turning sword at the entrance of the Garden of Eden to guard and protect the Tree of Life. Tomorrow will mark precisely one year since that fateful day when that Tree of Life was desecrated by the murderous rampage of an antisemitic gunman. Eleven of God's creation shot dead in Pittsburgh's Tree of Life synagogue, eleven souls who woke up that Shabbat morning seeking to do exactly what all of us in this room woke up seeking to do: connect to God, connect to community, and connect to our best selves. Eleven souls, members of three congregations, who wanted to heal our broken world by spending a morning in prayer, study, and fellowship, only to have that aim shattered forever by the murderous acts of a hate-filled gunman.

In the days following the Pittsburgh slaughter, our community came together, as did so many communities, in an outpouring of sorrow, solidarity, and outrage. A year has passed, and we remain shaken, the wound still fresh, the families still bereaved. If there is one thing I have learned as a rabbi, it is that nobody ever gets over loss; people just learn to manage it, one step, one day, at a time. For the families of the slain, for the Pittsburgh Jewish community, and for American Jewry, October 27, 2018 is a date that will be forever remembered, a wound that will never fully heal. For me as a congregational rabbi, the world is different: the precautions we take, the community conversations of which I am a part, and the budget dollars of Jewish institutions, this one included, now allocated to security. We all feel the ripple. Over the summer, when I go out of town and attend more modest synagogues, I find myself startled when I do *not* see a security guard. Taking my seat, I catch myself searching out where the emergency exits are located, and despite being Shabbat-observant, since that day I carry a cell phone in synagogue – just in case. The assumptions of American Jewry changed that day. We are still post-traumatic; though not always visible, our unease is altogether present. This weekend, in partnership with synagogues across the country and the AJC's #ShowUpForShabbat, we observe the one-year anniversary since the bloodshed, but the calendar marker is ultimately arbitrary. We are changed – today, tomorrow, and forever.

This morning, I would like to organize my reflections on the Tree of Life massacre under four headings, four baskets of reflection, in an attempt to put into words some of the harsh realities, lessons learned, and ongoing obligations that have emerged from that fateful day.

Lesson #1: Antisemitism. One year later, there is a temptation to reflect back on the murderous events of October 27 and extract some global lesson of universal application. That the root cause of the horror is a general deficit of civility or a general toxicity of our public discourse. No question we live in a time of escalating hatreds that need to be checked before they are weaponized as they were that horrific day. And yet, we dare not take our eye off the ball and lose sight of the headline: Antisemitism. It wasn't a refugee center, a civil rights organization, or an institution representing any one political leaning or interest. It was a synagogue – the building in American life most associated with Jews, the place where one goes if one wants to meet Jews . . . or kill them. Yes, we are blessed to live in a time and place where the state-sanctioned antisemitism of other times and places is not our experience. But antisemitism is real; it is present; it comes from the right and from the left. Not just in Poway, not just in Europe, but all over America. According to the ADL, over 50 Jewish institutions have been targeted since that day in Pittsburgh. We have witnessed the inability of Congress to call out antisemitism, choosing instead a watered-down resolution condemning discrimination in general. Just across the river, there have been a rising number of antisemitic assaults in the Jewish community of Brooklyn. You personally may not feel it, but it is there – on campus, on the internet, and across our country – the world's oldest hatred alive and well, a virus taking on new and more nefarious expressions, the bloodshed in Pittsburgh being the most violent but far from an exceptional incident.

One year later, the blood of our brothers and sisters cries out to us. We dare not lose our sense of outrage. In recalling the dead, some add *Y'hi zikronam barukh*, May their memories be for a blessing, while others say *Hamakom yikom damam*, May God avenge their blood. There are some who interpret the latter to mean that we must take vengeance – an eye for an eye. There are others who say it means that only God can exact vengeance, not human beings. I take it to mean, as our parashah teaches, that we dare not stand by idly as the blood of our kinsfolk is shed. We must lobby officials for public funding of security of our Jewish institutions, lest our synagogues and schools be forced to choose, because of the deeds of antisemites, between hiring teachers or guards. Of course we should support communal efforts to strengthen our social fabric – like the city's recently launched office to prevent hate crimes – but as a Jewish community we have a particular obligation to engage in our own parochial well-being. We have to resist the urge to let the status quo become a new normal. We have to keep our public officials accountable; we have to advocate on behalf of law enforcement authorities tasked to fight antisemitism; and we must provide support, in word and deed, to organizations like the ADL and the AJC whose sole mission is to protect the interests of the Jewish community. Lesson #1: antisemitism is alive and well, and our fight must be steadfast.

Lesson #2: Look for the helpers. Before the Tree of Life shooting, most Americans associated the Pittsburgh neighborhood of Squirrel Hill with its most famous resident, Mister Rogers, the icon who famously reminded us that in the face of tragedy one must "look for the helpers," a point made clear in a recent article by Pittsburgh native Nancy Strichman. (*The Times of Israel*, October 19, 2019) I think of police officers like Dan Mead, the first responder who was shot as he entered Tree of Life that day. I think of the millions of dollars raised to assist those traumatized by the shooting. I think of the hundreds of thousands raised by the Muslim community alone. I think of the civic response by the Pittsburgh community, the support of the Pittsburgh Steelers who changed their logo in support of the victims. I think of the thousands of people who came to Pittsburgh from across the country for funerals and memorial services, who rallied together in crisis, the evil intentions of one person prompting so many kind acts.

To be sure, by looking for the helpers, we risk diverting ourselves from the horror, seeking a Hollywood silver lining in what should be known only as an unmitigated atrocity. No question, focusing on the good does not bring back lost lives or heal shattered families. Nevertheless, in recalling acts of kindness performed in the wake of the massacre, we are reminded that a humanity capable of senseless hatred also has the capacity to perform acts of selfless kindness. Is this not the message that God gives to Cain and all of subsequent humanity? That every human being is capable of doing both good and evil, that each one of us can choose kindness, reaching deeper and striving higher in our efforts to mend our broken world. It is a shame that it takes a tragedy to prompt us to look for the helpers; we should do it year-round, celebrating and elevating the manifold acts of kindness that bind us together as humanity.

Lesson #3: Choose Life. Married as I am to a daughter of Squirrel Hill, I know many of the people and players, lay and professional, who lead Pittsburgh's Jewish community. That said, I can't even begin to imagine the financial, emotional, and institutional considerations going into the future of Tree of Life synagogue, still shuttered one year later. Should the building, pockmarked by bullet holes, be razed? Should Pittsburghers, as would Israelis following a terrorist attack, close the building for an afternoon, repaint the walls, and open for business the next day? Should it be turned into a museum honoring the dead and the martyrs of other atrocities committed against the Jewish people – the Holocaust included? These are a few of the options presently being debated by Pittsburgh Jewry. But the question is not just about the physical building. It is a philosophical question. What should be the path forward in the wake of the tragedy?

To be clear, I am not of the opinion voiced by some that the only response to Pittsburgh is to live Jewishly. We have to fight antisemitism at its root and in all its expressions: verbal, physical, online, and otherwise. As I indicated on the High Holidays, the fact of antisemitism – ancient or modern – is not a compelling reason to live a joyous Jewish life. But I do believe that as Jews we are obligated to muster the requisite resilience of soul to do what those eleven souls sought to do on that final Shabbat morning of their lives: live quiet, proud, dignified Jewish lives of meaning. We must choose life. I am reminded of the midrash regarding creation, about God who found the spiritual wherewithal to create our world after experiencing setback. It wouldn't be the worst thing in the world were you to live Jewishly if only to thumb your nose at antisemites. But ultimately, we need to live proud Jewish lives not because people have tried, are trying, and will try to do us harm. We need to live proud and joyful Jewish lives because it is our right, privilege, and obligation to do so. We need to do so because, like those slain, we believe in the power of the Jewish people and the role of a synagogue to inspire, educate, and support its membership toward living passion-filled Jewish lives. We need to choose life.

Fourth, finally and most obviously – we need to remember. We need to pause today to meditate on the lives lost that day, each one a universe of his or her own. I think of the decision of each of those Jews to go to synagogue that morning, the connection each of them had to their God, their tradition, and their community. I did not know any of them personally, I imagine most of us did not. I imagine them to be the sort of folk in shul on any given Shabbat morning. This one sitting by the door greeting the newcomer, maybe pointing out the page number in the prayer book. Another sitting on his own, contemplating a life transition, perhaps observing a yahrzeit or celebrating an anniversary. This one trying her best to keep to her Rosh Hashanah resolution to be more engaged in Jewish life by coming to shul every week. This one comes every week, constantly kvetching, always sharing how great the shul would be if only the rabbi would listen to his input. We may not know them, but we are them, and we remember them, our kin who were slain:

> Joyce Fienberg
> Richard Gottfried
> Rose Mallinger
> Jerry Rabinowitz
> Cecil Rosenthal
> David Rosenthal
> Bernice Simon
> Sylvan Simon
> Daniel Stein
> Melvin Wax
> Irving Young

Our brothers and sisters, gunned down for no reason other than their decision to do what all of us are doing – attend synagogue on a Shabbat morning.

It is one year later. Today we stand outside the garden of our innocence, never to return. The Tree of Life has been violated. Our sense of security, if we ever had it, is no more. We step forward into a world far more frightening than we ever thought possible. May we heal, may we find our way, and most of all, today and always, may we remember those slain one year ago.

Y'hi zikhronam barukh, May their memories be for a blessing. *Hamakom yikom damam*, May God avenge their blood. Please rise for the memorial prayer.

October 26, 2019
27 Tishrei 5780

Strichman, Nancy, "Looking and learning from the helpers," *Times of Israel*, October 19, 2019
https://blogs.timesofisrael.com/looking-and-learning-from-the-helpers

Noaḥ
The Anxiety of Influence

If there is one phrase associated with Harold Bloom, who passed away last month at the age of 89, it is "the anxiety of influence." Born in the Bronx to an Orthodox Jewish household, Bloom went on to become the most prodigious literary critic of the twentieth century. His love affair with literature took him from devouring anthologies of Yiddish poetry to a mastery of the Western canon at Cornell and then to Yale, where he would receive his doctorate and then teach throughout his career. I never knew Bloom personally, but as a literature major at Michigan, it was impossible not to encounter him. His studies on Shakespeare, Montaigne, Whitman, Emerson, Marvell, and so many others made Bloom a steady companion, guide, and sometimes foil in my own studies. Bloom's influence went beyond the ivory tower as he shared his love of literature with a broad readership by way of bestsellers. I remember the stir surrounding his 1990 *The Book of J*, in which Bloom unpacks the historical context of one strand of biblical authorship, suggesting the author to be a woman in the royal court of King Solomon. Prolific, provocative, and not without personal controversy, Bloom was a giant of literary criticism.

Bloom's most famous book *The Anxiety of Influence*, was published in 1973. In it, Bloom outlines his theory of intra-poetic relationships, in other words, how one poet influences another. As all of us intuitively understand, no poet emerges in a vacuum. Virgil had his Homer just as Dante had his Virgil. Shakespeare had Marlowe; Emerson had Montaigne; Spenser had Chaucer; and so on and so forth. No different than Monet influenced Cezanne and Cezanne influenced Matisse,

Picasso, and others; no different than Guthrie influenced Dylan who influenced Springsteen. Every art form – music, painting, architecture and poetry – reflects a process of influence that can be studied and traced. But for Bloom, this observation is just the beginning of a discussion of poetic influence. Because while every poet is, by definition, subject to influence, every poet also aspires to assert him- or herself as original. The "anxiety of influence" is the poet's struggle (*agon* in Bloom's language), to be an extension of their predecessors and at the same time, overcome, sublimate, redirect, or reject that influence. According to Bloom, the measure of a poet – and for Bloom the world is divided into strong and weak poets – is the degree to which they are able to master their poetic forebears, overcome them, and, in rare cases, transcend them to create something truly new.

If you think this sounds very Freudian, you are right. And if you think this sounds very rabbinic, then you are right on that front, too. Bloom himself identified Freud as one of two prime influences upon him (the other being Nietzsche). That's unsurprising given that his entire thesis hangs on the notion that great literature reflects a sort of Oedipal attempt of a writer to surmount the life-giving parent-poet. (*Anxiety of Influence*, p. 8) In a later book, Bloom reflects that the rabbinic project of midrash and kabbalah is akin to one writer reading and sometimes misreading a prior writer in order to emerge with an original reading – a process, in Bloom's words, suggestive of the kabbalistic concept of *shevirat kelim*, in which the primordial vessels of creation must be broken in order to be restored. That is a sermon for another day – a fascinating reading of the rabbinic project as the attempt of every Jewish generation to be both an extension of and a reaction to the generation that came before. It leaves us wondering how much Bloom's Jewish background may have influenced the very theory of influence for which he became famous.

While all of this is of interest, in order to understand the possible Jewish influences on Bloom's theory of influence, one need look no further than this morning's Torah reading, concluding with the introduction of our people's founding forefather, Abraham. The origin story of the Jewish people is typically thought to begin *next* week when

Abram is called on by God to go forth from his land to the land that God will show him. You may have missed that it is actually today, in the final verses of *this* week's Torah reading that we meet Abram, as Abraham was originally known. If you read closely, you will discover that Abraham's famed journey begins not with Abraham, but with Abraham's father Teraḥ, or more precisely, with Teraḥ's father, who died in Ur Kasdim. Upon his father's death, Teraḥ took his son Abram, Abram's wife Sarai, and the whole family from Ur Kasdim to Canaan by way of Haran, where Teraḥ himself would pass. It is only then, at the point where next week's Torah reading begins, that Abraham is called on by God to leave his homeland in order to go to the land that God will show him. It is an odd command if you consider that Abraham had left his birthplace long before and was already on his way to Canaan. It is a bit complicated, but the takeaway is there for all to see: Abraham's story did not begin with him, it began with his father. His journey, geographically and spiritually, is an extension of what came before.

I know . . . that is not the story you learned in Hebrew school. And I know, this reading lacks the drama of how we have liked to imagine Abraham – a breaker of idols, an original and true iconoclast. But it is a telling that is true to the text. All we know for certain about Abraham's early years is that he followed, quite literally, in his father's formidable footstePsalm Abraham's call from God was thus his opportunity to affirm the journey of his father, but in his own way: both an extension of and a reaction to that which came before. Abraham is Abraham not because he broke with the past, nor because he continued on his father's path. Abraham is who he is because he struggled mightily with the anxiety of influence and emerged as a product of his predecessors and was also an original the likes of which our world had never seen. A traditional reading? Perhaps not, but a reading, I submit to you, that is true to the plain meaning of the text and true to what we know to be the case in our own lives.

While this anxiety of influence is first seen in this morning's recounting of Abraham's relationship with his father Teraḥ, it does not end there. Some time after Abraham emerges from the shadow of his father, he and Sarah are finally blessed with the birth of Isaac. Born for the express purpose of actualizing God's covenant with his father, Isaac is famously brought to the top of Mount Moriah to be sacrificed by Abraham at God's command – a Freudian father-son psychoanalytic drama if ever there was one. That near-death event understandably prompts Isaac to part ways with his father, but the text relates that soon after Abraham's passing, Isaac uncovered the wells his father had dug, an act that the Rabbis acknowledge as a recovery of Abraham's legacy by his estranged son.

The pattern continues with Isaac's son Jacob, who, due to a combination of clumsy parenting and regrettable sibling rivalry, first acquires his father's blessing and then flees his father's house. The story of Jacob is also a story of the anxiety of influence, a man who at one and the same time seeks his father's approval, all the while trying to establish his own personhood, as like his father as he is unlike. The exact same tension is, not surprisingly, found in Jacob's son Joseph. Joseph, who dreams like his father Jacob, is identified explicitly as his father's favorite but ultimately has to leave his father's home in order to grow into the man he dreams of being. This week's and next week's Torah readings are the kick-off to the patriarchal narratives, in which every protagonist struggles to embrace their predecessor while staking out new territory. This anxiety of influence is the narrative thread that holds the book of Genesis together. It is not just the men, the fathers and sons. Similar anxieties can be found in the lives of Rebecca, Rachel, Leah, and especially Dina – all women who define themselves as an extension of their households of origin and also reach beyond them. If you think about it – if you really think about it – this tension actually begins prior to Abraham. Not just when Adam raised a Cain, but in the Garden of Eden itself. What is the story of Creation if not the tale of a humanity created in the image of God the parent, a humanity who, from the very start, seek to assert themselves, even if – especially if – it means breaking with that very One who granted the gift of life in the first place.

I have the good fortune of having about as good a relationship with my old man as I could ask for: He loves me; he looks out for me;

and he lets me be. I treasure our relationship. I am well aware how lucky I am, and I hope to be a father to my children in the way that my father is to me. If I experience an anxiety of influence, it is not from my father, but in relationship to my grandfather I never knew, also a congregational rabbi, whose extended shadow shelters, shapes, and guides me even as I try to emerge from under it. All of us exist under an anxiety of influence of one sort or another – our mothers, our fathers, our siblings, our teachers, our mentors, biologically related or not, whether we knew them or not. We would not be here without them; we are who we are because of them; and yet we become our fullest selves only when we escape their gravitational pull and define our identities on our own terms. It is the struggle that defines who we are and sets the course for our lives. There is no shortage of reasons why the book of Genesis continues to have a millenia-long hold on its readers, but maybe the most potent is that it reminds us that none of us is an original, no matter what we may believe. The text and subtext of all our lives, like the lives of the figures we read about during these weeks, are written under the anxiety of influence.

One final image: There is a beautiful and enigmatic rabbinic midrash, a parable told about Abraham's origins, comparing Abraham's "aha moment" to that of a man who sees a house full of light (in Hebrew, *doleket*), and is prompted to ask, "Is it possible that the house has no owner?" In answer, the owner of the house peers out and declares, "I am the owner." Some interpret the midrash to mean that Abraham saw a world aflame and on the brink of ruin, and Abraham's greatness was that he took on the responsibility to save God's world. Others, including Rabbi Abraham Joshua Heschel, interpret the midrash to mean that Abraham was thunderstruck by the light of creation, and Abraham's greatness was his ability to understand from the wonder and beauty of creation that there must be a single God of the cosmos.

Under the influence not of Harold Bloom, but an even more modern prophet of father-son relationships, Bruce Springsteen, I choose to interpret the midrash as follows: The man in the house on fire is not meant to be God. The man in that house filled with light is

Teraḥ; the house – is Teraḥ's house, the house that Abraham left. In Bruce's lyrics: ". . . that shines hard and bright. It stands like a beacon calling [him] in the night." Abraham has left home and yet yearns to return. His father's presence beckons even as a full homecoming is forever beyond reach. Abraham stands, as do we all, balancing the debt we hold to those who gave us life against our ongoing efforts to transcend them. It is the anxiety that defines us, the tension that shapes us, and ultimately – redemptively – the struggle that gives us strength and offers us the possibility of unlocking our heroic potential.

November 2, 2019
4 Heshvan 5780

Va-yera
Bystanders and Upstanders

If you have never heard of Kazimierz Sakowicz, don't worry; neither had I until three days ago. For the past ten days, together with 120 congregants and under the leadership of Rabbi Savenor, I participated in a congregational trip to St. Petersburg, Moscow and then, for about thirty of us, to Lithuania. I had never been to Vilna, the capital of Lithuania, where my great-grandparents and no doubt many of yours were born. Vilna: home to the eighteenth-century rabbinic giant the Vilna Gaon; once the center of all Jewish learning, the "Jerusalem of Lithuania." Vilna: a glorious history that came to a horrific end at the hands of the Nazis during the Holocaust. On June 24, 1941, just days after the beginning of Operation Barbarossa, the Nazis entered Lithuania. Shortly thereafter, with the arrival of the *Einsatzkommando* – the German killing brigade – the roundup of Lithuanian Jews began in earnest. On July 11, the first group of Jews were marched into the Ponary Forest to be killed, the start of a prolonged massacre that by its conclusion about two years later had claimed 100,000 lives, of which 70,000 were Jews. The mass killing ended not owing to mercy but just the opposite. Having calculated the economics of 1.5 bullets per dead Jew, the Nazis sought a more cost-efficient path toward achieving their murderous goals, which led to the establishment of concentration camps, gas chambers, and crematoria. Standing at the site of the mass graves in the Ponary Forest earlier this week was to stand at ground zero for the depths to which humanity can sink, as sad and sobering an experience as I have had in all my days.

What we know about Ponary we know by way of scraps of testimony from survivors and perpetrators, and none is more important than the diary of Kazimierz Sakowicz. Sakowicz was a Polish journalist who lived in the village adjacent to Ponary Forest. From that very first evening of July 11, 1941, Sakowicz chronicled the atrocities as he observed them from a hiding place in his attic and in the of testimony of others. Aware of the risks in recording the crimes around him, he hid his notes in lemonade bottles buried in the ground. We will never know what Sakowicz intended to do with his diaries. Sakowicz was killed in unclear circumstances in July 1944; his diaries were not found until after the war and were not translated into English until the 1990s. (K. Sakowicz, *Ponary Diary: A Bystander's Account of a Mass Murder*, ed. Y. Arad, 2005)

Sakowicz was no saint. I read the diary this week, and there is something jarring about the matter-of-fact manner in which he relates the murderous actions of the Nazis alongside the weather of the day, as well as how he records his scorn for the Jewish victims. But for me, the take-home of Sakowicz's diary is not Sakowicz, nor for that matter the Nazi atrocities with which we in this room are well familiar. What I found most disturbing about Sakowicz's chronicle was his characterization of the local Lithuanian population – the accomplices, collaborators, and bystanders to the mass killing. The inhumanity of the Nazis was not news, but I was struck by the way that locals stood by as the victims were led to the pits, ignoring their pleas, in some cases doing the shooting themselves, covering the victims with dirt after stripping them of their clothing, and carrying away their belongings to be traded in the marketplace. Not one or two nights, not one or two months, but for nearly two years, and there is no record of any moral objection. An entire community was complicit in a moral outrage. Nobody stepped up to intercede in the face of what must rank as one of the most inhumane chapters of human history.

Of all the indicators by which moral behavior can be measured, none is as clear, in its breach or fulfillment, as the willingness of an individual to put themselves on the line on behalf of another. It is laudable and praiseworthy, no question, to act in self-defense and care for one's own well-being. So too, one should always strive to champion and defend the values one holds dear. But for Jews, moral behavior goes a step further. Moral stature is measured not merely by how we defend self-interest, nor for that matter by our support for certain ideals in times of comfort. We are measured by our willingness – or in the case of the Lithuanians, unwillingness – to intercede on behalf of another, even when, if not especially when, doing so puts our own interests at risk.

We need look no further than this morning's Torah reading and the actions of our people's founder Abraham to see this moral standard given expression. Having been granted a covenant by God in the form of land, blessing, and progeny, Abraham is given advance warning of God's intention to destroy the wicked cities of Sodom and Gomorrah. In a move as bold as it is courageous, Abraham steps up to intercede on behalf of people that he neither knows nor knows to be worthy of an impassioned defense. "Will You sweep away the innocent with the guilty?" Abraham remonstrates. What if there are fifty, forty-five, forty, twenty, ten righteous people found? Will you, God, still carry out your destruction? The significance of the narrative is not whether Abraham was successful; he was not. Nor for our purposes today is it important to understand the mysteries of divine justice. The significance of the exchange as noted by the Jewish mystical text the Zohar is that Abraham's willingness to go toe-to-toe with God illustrates his moral stature. Unlike Noah, who, when informed of God's plan to wipe out the entire human race, went ahead with building an ark to save himself, his family, and a bunch of animals, Abraham risks all, beseeching God to restrain the divine wrath directed at the inhabitants of Sodom.

The circumstances and players of our Torah reading are as different from the aforementioned chapter of Holocaust history as night is from day, but the moral muscle group is one and the same. And it is not just this one scene. Throughout the Bible, the willingness or failure of one individual to stand up for another is the litmus test, the moral thread that holds our biblical narrative together. From Cain standing by the blood of Abel to Joseph's brothers standing by as their brother is left in the pit to die to Judah placing himself at risk on behalf of his brother Benjamin to Moses striking down the Egyptian as an Israelite slave is beaten or, more famously, stepping into the breach as the Israelites stand guilty before God for the sin of the golden calf, in each of these instances and so many others, the moral highs and lows of our people are found in an individual's standing up for another. This intercessory instinct, taught my late teacher, Dr. Yochanan Muffs, is the mark of a prophet and hero for our people. As *Pirkei Avot*, the Ethics of Our Fathers, teaches: "In a place where there are no upstanders, strive to be an upstander." (2:5)

We could leave it at that. But those who know what happens next, in the two scenes following Sodom and Gomorrah, know that soon enough our heroic Abraham is cast in an altogether different light. Our stand-up guy, it turns out, is not always the stand-up guy we would expect him to be. First, as we read on Rosh Hashanah, Abraham stands by silently as Hagar and Ishmael are expelled from his home. Where, we may ask, is our heroic intercessor now? And then, more famously, in the following chapter, God calls on Abraham to sacrifice his son Isaac, a gut-wrenching request to which Abraham accedes all too willingly. How is it possible that the bold hero who interceded on behalf of Sodom now stands silent when it comes to his own flesh and blood? What has become of Abraham's moral stature?

It is a question and conundrum that is perplexing not just to me and you, but to generations of biblical commentators. Why the two Abrahams – the morally heroic and the morally meek. How do we square the circle of our founding father, who over the course of such a short time displays such utterly contradictory character traits? While centuries of rabbis have proposed a variety of answers seeking to recast, excuse, or mitigate Abraham's behavior, this year I see it differently. This year I would suggest that the point is not in resolving or reconciling the conflict, but in the fact of the conflict itself. I believe the whole point is that we, the reader, are provided, over the course of a few chapters, with one person, Abraham, offering multiple responses to the call to be an upstander, the central test of biblical morality.

Simply put, I think the message of the Torah is that every human being, even the great ones like Abraham, can on any given day be pulled one way or another. None of us lives with the weighty inflection points of our biblical forebears, or, thank God, the decision-making of those complicit in the genocidal acts of the twentieth century. But all of us do live in a world every bit as morally gray as it was on that first day that God created it; and we in this room are living through a moral free fall the likes of which I cannot recall in my lifetime. Each one of us, every day, is faced with a series of decisions – momentous and mundane – that call on us to differentiate right from wrong and choose one path or another. And a certain percentage of those choices will involve not our own well-being, but our willingness to intercede on behalf of others. And then a subset of those decisions will involve us interceding on behalf of another in a manner that calls on us to risk our own well-being – social, financial, political, and sometimes physical.

It is not a traditional read of the text by any stretch, but I believe the Torah intentionally provides us with instances when Abraham got it right – like Sodom and Gomorrah – and instances when Abraham got it wrong – like Hagar and Ishmael and the binding of Isaac. Had the Torah done otherwise, had it given us a one-dimensional Abraham who always got it right, his function as a moral exemplar would cease because his level of moral excellence would be unattainable. We need examples of both his success and his failure because we need to know that for each of us, as for Abraham, nobody gets it right every time. All of us struggle, and it is in that struggle and in the knowledge that others have struggled that we find our strength. We need to keep trying; we need to keep aspiring toward our potential heroic stature, even if on occasion we fail, even when it is hard, and especially when it seems out of reach. We dare not have the annals of history look back at us, as we do at past generations, wondering how was it that good people just stood by silently in the face of evil.

That day in Lithuania began with Sakowicz, and it ended with someone named Sugihara. As we returned to the city from Ponary Forest, we stopped briefly at a memorial built in honor of Chiune Sugihara, a diplomat sent by the Japanese government to open a consulate in Lithuania. Recognizing the dangers faced by Lithuanian Jewry, over a period of just a few months, ignoring the orders of the Japanese Foreign Ministry, Sugihara issued visa after visa enabling Jews to travel the Trans-Siberian Railway to the port of Vladivostok, where they boarded ships bound for Kobe, Japan and then to Shanghai, and then, eventually, after the war, to safety. Sugihara worked desperate twenty-hour days saving as many Jews as he could, until, under pressure, he himself was forced to leave. To the very last minute, he issued visas, in the lobby as he packed up, and according to witnesses, up to and including the moment he threw blank signed visas out the window of the train as it pulled away. A midlevel Japanese diplomat with no connection to Jews, Sugihara issued some 10,000 visas. Today there are over 40,000 descendants of the Jews saved by the actions of one man, who because of those actions was demoted after the war by the foreign ministry, taking a series of menial jobs and reduced at one point to selling light bulbs door-to-door. It was not until 1984 that Yad Vashem recognized him as a Righteous Among the Nations – to date, the only Japanese recipient of that honor. (Hillel Levine, *In Search of Sugihara*, 1996)

And I stood at the Sugihara memorial, I wondered why Sugihara did what he did. Why does anyone do what they do? According to one account, the only explanation Sugihara offered was: "I acted according to my sense of human justice, out of love for mankind." (Levine, p. 282) The very simplicity of Sugihara's response is instructive and inspiring for us all today.

None of us is perfect, and none of us, not even Abraham, gets it right all the time. But a common person, you or I, can perform acts of uncommon good. In response to challenge, we can all be elevated beyond what we think ourselves capable of, what we think possible. Moral heroism is not reserved just for biblical figures. It is there for all of us, in all our ordinariness, to the extent we are willing to step up to the calling of the hour.

November 16, 2019
18 Ḥeshvan 5780

Va-yiggash
Time to Step Up and March

Aside from the out-of-town guests of this morning's bnei mitzvah, whose travel plans may prevent them from joining tomorrow's "No Hate. No Fear." solidarity march, I imagine that most everyone in this room is actively thinking about whether or not they should attend Sunday's planned rally in Brooklyn.

If by some chance you have not yet heard, received an email, or read the editorials in *The New York Times* and elsewhere, tomorrow morning the Jewish and non-Jewish community together will meet at Foley Square at 11:00 am and march across the Brooklyn Bridge to Cadman Plaza – a communal response to the rash of antisemitic incidents and attacks that have afflicted our community this past month.

The facts are as startling as they are alarming. Thirteen reported attacks in New York in December, and that does not include the Jersey City attack that killed three. Incidents every night of the just-completed festival of Hanukkah, including last Saturday night's horrific attack in Monsey. This is not Europe or some distant yesteryear; this is your city, our city – our "I Heart NY" home – shaken to its multicultural core. The New York Jewish community is on high alert; law enforcement has been deployed; and resources are being mobilized.

Last night at Kabbalat Shabbat we heard from Mitchell Silber, the incoming director of New York City's newly created Community Security Initiative. Next Friday evening we will hear from Deborah Lauter, Director of the NYC Office for the Prevention of Hate Crimes. The synagogue has signed on to interfaith calls to action; we are participants in the synagogue initiative of the Anti-Defamation League, whose National Director and CEO, Jonathan Greenblatt, spoke here last month. Rabbi Zuckerman is working with our lay leadership to craft our evolving communal response. Next week I will be traveling to Rome for a Vatican meeting on how the global religious community can be mobilized in the fight against hate. Members of this PAS community should be touched by the number of my local clergy colleagues who have reached out to me personally, offering words of comfort and support.

Please be assured that the security and safety of our congregants and staff has always been and continues to be the highest priority for the leadership of PAS. While the rest of the world may be slowly waking up to the realities of this new year, you should know that your synagogue is fully alert and responsive to the emerging landscape.

And yet, when it comes to tomorrow's community-wide march, I sense hesitation. As I have worked the phones, read my emails, and spoken with folks these last two days, to the degree that I can measure these things, I have not yet heard a full-throated commitment. I am not convinced that the urgency of the hour and the need to show up is felt fully or felt by all.

Some of the hesitation comes, understandably, from concern regarding safety and security. There are those who wonder if a public spectacle of outrage is the most prudent course of action at this time. Now, they say, is the time to lay low and not draw attention to ourselves. To escalate with a rally is neither politically expedient nor physically safe. God knows what can happen in this charged environment.

Alternatively, there are those who are wondering, a little more benignly, what good does a rally do anyway? Rallies are the political instruments of yesteryear. "I care deeply," they say, "about the scourge of antisemitism, which is why I post on social media, why I sit on boards of communal Jewish organizations, why I write checks. I care . . . but it's cold, it's football Sunday and, well, I already gave at the office."

Dynamics of the rally aside, if you scratch beneath the surface, some of the hesitation goes to the heart of the issue: the nature of the antisemitism itself. Some question whether the "sky is falling" narrative of the return of antisemitism is not a little overstated. It was not lost on me that the same *Jewish Week* edition that covered the attack in Jersey City also contained a lead article on the rededication of our own synagogue – a statement of the vitality of New York Jewish life if there ever was one. Is this the best of times or the worst of times for the Jews of New York? I could, and I imagine you could, make the argument both ways. Besides, some may say: "Antisemitism is the oldest and most persistent hatred. This is nothing new. A synagogue should devote its energy to building Jewish identity. Let the ADL take point on this one."

There are also those who have said and written that this hatred is not actually about the Jews. Rather, it is a symptom of a societal malady felt by all – a social ill that is not about Jews but about something much deeper – a loss of civility reflecting social and economic anxiety and uncertainty. Just five days ago, there was a church shooting in Texas – nothing to do with Jews, nothing to do with New York. Our attention is better directed at gun control, at political change, at tighter borders, at more porous borders, at education, at mental health, or maybe toward building bridges to communities for whom the Jewish community needs to be demystified. Antisemitism is just a symptom, and a rally is no antidote for the systemic disease that lurks beneath.

Part of the hesitation, I imagine, is rooted in a bit of confusion. I myself have a hard time piecing it all together. Swastikas on synagogues smack of a resurgence of right-wing neo-Nazism. Jersey City's attacker was a Black Hebrew Israelite. Monsey's attacker had a mental health history; it is not so clear what prompted him, and it may never be. Given the world events of the last forty-eight hours, our most pressing concern may actually be from a radicalized Muslim community. And not every attack against a Jew is necessarily antisemitic. It wasn't New York, but you may have heard of the incident at a college campus last week in which some Jewish students were beaten up by other students. The attack was labeled antisemitic, the incident shared widely. When I asked my nephew, who attended that university, he explained that it was a bunch of drunk college kids – an idiotic intra-fraternity party-crashing fistfight. I am sure Deborah Lauter will speak directly to the topic next Friday evening: When is a crime a hate crime? When is an attack against a Jew antisemitic? Are all antisemitisms equal and equally threatening? The answers are not entirely clear.

And while we are probing the guts of our communal response to antisemitism, let's poke at some of the really uncomfortable questions. The outrage of the non-Orthodox community has no doubt been tempered by the question of to what degree attacks on the ultra-Orthodox community are actually attacks on us. Most of us have very few contacts, family members, and close friends in the ultra-Orthodox community. They dress differently; they attend different schools; they lead insular, separate lives. It is not just that they are siloed from us and we from them. Their Judaism is different from ours, and our Judaism is not Judaism to them. Three weeks from today we will be having our annual Shabbaton, devoted this year to an exploration of the future of synagogue life. We have a great line-up, but I also really wanted the views of a non-liberal rabbi, so I invited a Chabad rabbi of some repute. He told me point-blank that he would not speak here because to do so would "legitimate" (his precise word) me and my synagogue. God forbid, God forbid! But if something should happen to his community, how do I mobilize my community in support of a rabbi and a community who does not see my Judaism as Judaism and my Jews as Jews?

You and I both know that the internal divisions of the Jewish community fall not only along the religious spectrum but the political as well. We are living in a painful time when those holding the loudest megaphones in our community are spending more time pointing fingers at each other than at the antisemites themselves. As fast as the political left castigates the right for trafficking in classic antisemitic tropes about Jews – financial self-interest and dual loyalty – the political right is quick to point out the very same sins on the progressive left. Both sides claim to be prompted by Jewish values and interests; neither side has totally clean hands; unholy alliances have been made by all. It is mind-boggling and altogether depressing to consider the energy that has been expended stoking division among Jews as the noxious fumes of antisemitism pollute our society.

There are and will always be reasons to hesitate, to hedge, to stay silent, and to sit the round out. Lest we forget, the central drama of this morning's Torah reading revolves around the question of whether Judah will step up at the moment that the fate of his brother Benjamin hangs in the balance. Judah had a million reasons to stay silent – his own self-preservation being the most obvious. Did he have any assurances that stepping up would not cause his downfall – or possibly the downfall of his brother or of all his brothers? As our *Etz Hayim* commentary notes, Judah knew the underbelly of fraternal rivalry and the sting of his father's favoritism. Why should he stand up for Benjamin? What did he care for his father's feelings – a father who had repeatedly slighted him? Why should he step up and stick his neck out for them?

But as you know, as I know, Judah does step up. At the very moment when Judah had a million reasons to keep his head down, he does what he didn't do when Joseph was first thrown into the pit, what Jacob didn't do for Esau, what Isaac and Ishmael couldn't do for each other, what Cain couldn't do for Abel, what no biblical brother had done thus far: He stood up for his brother. In fact, as my colleague Rabbi Charlie Savenor has insightfully pointed out in a commentary on MyJewishLearning.com, Judah's action may be understood as a rejoinder to the beginning of Genesis, to Cain, who asked, *Hashomer aḥi anokhi*, Am I my brother's keeper? (Genesis 4:9) It is here, when Judah steps up on behalf of his brother, that Judah becomes Judah, worthy of his name – emphatically his brother's keeper and the father of our people and nation.

It is Judah's willingness to step up, one sibling for another, even when – especially when – there may be reasons not to, that make you and me Judah's descendants: Jews.

I urge the members of this community to show up for the march and rally tomorrow because that is what Jews do for each other when someone is hurting, when someone is in danger, when someone is in need. We show up. To a shiva house, to make a minyan, for Israel, for Soviet Jewry. In our religion simply showing up is a commandment, a *mitzvah*, and tomorrow is a time for that *mitzvah*.

I urge you to show up for the rally because I believe that now is exactly *not* the time to keep our heads down. Now is the time for a numerical show of political will. To announce that Jews will not be made to remove our yarmulkes in public. That Jews reject a world that makes us choose whether to hire another Jewish educator or a security guard. That no community should have to endure hatred, violence, or fear. That we demand that our government, law enforcement, and fellow citizens publicly and demonstrably come down hard against this epidemic of Jew hatred.

I urge you to you show up tomorrow because whatever you believe politically, now is the time to announce to the world that no matter what our internal fissures may be, we stand united as allies in the fight against antisemitism and hatred.

I urge you to show up tomorrow because I have never and will never live or lead this institution based on what someone else thinks of me. Two wrongs don't make a right. Do we really believe that in the eyes of the antisemite there is a difference between a Conservative synagogue in Pittsburgh and a Chabad in Poway? Antisemites do not make distinctions between Jews and neither should we.

I urge you to show up tomorrow because there is a time to intellectualize, and there is a time to act. Antisemitism may be the disease or it may be the symptom, but that symptom is killing Jews. I have no idea if this is the best of times or the worst of times, whether the events of the last month signal the opening of a new chapter or the return of an ancient hatred. We can all read the next article by Deborah Lipstadt or Abe Foxman. We can all debate where our philanthropic and political muscle is best directed. Those articles and debates and requests for your money will be there on Monday – I promise. Tomorrow is not about analysis. Tomorrow is about doing the one thing we can all do equally: Show up to announce to the world that antisemitism has no place in New York, in civil society, or in this world.

I urge you to show up tomorrow for a million reasons, but most of all because that is what one sibling does for another. No person bearing the pedigree of our patriarch Judah should ever stand idly by as Jewish blood is shed. As Judah came to understand at the critical hour, as Moses understood when he saw his brethren suffer under the Egyptian taskmaster, as Esther came to understand when the fate of the Jews of Persia hung in the balance, we step up. That is what we do. As taught in *Pirkei Avot*, The Ethics of our Fathers: "In a place where there are no upstanders, strive to be an upstander." (2:5)

Tomorrow morning, 11:00 am. *No Hate, No Fear*. Let's be upstanders together.

January 4, 2020
7 Tevet 5780

Savenor, Charles, "Joseph's Moment of Truth"
https://www.myjewishlearning.com/article/josephs-moment-of-truth

B'shallaḥ
Making Sense of Our Moment

For those of us trying to make sense of the challenges facing American Jewry in 2020 – antisemitism, anti-Zionism, BDS (boycotts, divestments and sanctions), intersectionality, and more – 1960 is as good a place to start as any. This morning, I want to focus on today, but I want to get to today by way of yesterday. Specifically, I want to focus on three events or movements anchored in the past, which together provide a prism through which to view the present and maybe, if you stick with me, provide direction forward into the future.

Event number one is eerily resonant given recent news. Sixty years ago, in January 1960, – a swastika epidemic broke out across Europe. First, a newly rededicated synagogue in Cologne, Germany was vandalized with swastikas, antisemitic graffiti and the words *Juden Raus*, Out with the Jews, scrawled on the walls. But, as James Loeffler explains in his book, *Rooted Cosmopolitans: Jews and Human Rights in the Twentieth Century*, Cologne was just the beginning. In the days, weeks, and months that followed, synagogues and Jewish communal buildings were vandalized throughout Western Germany and in London, Antwerp, Vienna, Paris, and New York. Swastikas appeared in East Germany and Latin America, in Hong Kong, Algeria, and South Africa. By the end of 1960, the total had climbed to some 2,500 incidents in over forty countries.

Historians now know that the swastika epidemic began as a Soviet effort to discredit West Germany in the eyes of the west, a fact then unknown to Jews and unimportant to the many antisemitic copycats.

The epidemic prompted outrage, condemnation, calls to action, and, no doubt, fear. Think about how we, an empowered American Jewry of 2020, react to the appearance of swastikas. I shudder to imagine the impact of this outburst of antisemitism on the global Jewish psyche just fifteen years after the Holocaust. Had the world learned nothing? Would Jews ever be safe? How would the world respond to this virus of Judeophobia? With the epidemic in full swing, Maurice Perlzweig of the World Jewish Congress called for international action, a UN resolution condemning "manifestations of anti-Semitism," a story to which to we shall return soon enough.

But 1960 was not just the year of the swastika epidemic; for the global community, it was best known as "The Year of Africa," the second 1960 event on our list of three. Fifteen years before, Africa had been nearly entirely under colonial rule. Decolonization and the declaration of new states in the 1950s brought a new geopolitical reality and also an international consensus that human rights would be defined not only as protection of the individual from the abuses of state power, but also as the right of people to national self-determination. This assertion grew, in Loeffler's words, into a vehicle "for anticolonial nationalism." With respect to the emerging Soviet/Arab/Afro-Caribbean alignment, the international community was committed to "the right of self-determination," with one notable exception: the Jewish people. In the eyes of the global community, Israel – far from reflecting the multi-millennial Jewish hope for self-determination – was an extension of Western imperialism.

An all-out assault on Israel began at the UN in the name of anti-colonialism. When the Israeli delegate, Michael Comay, lodged a complaint about the omission of antisemitism from the resolution being drafted in response to the swastika epidemic, the UN representative from Mauritania blasted "Zionist expansionism" as the antithesis of human rights, unperturbed both by the fact that his country still permitted legal slavery, and that whatever his animus may have been against the Jewish state, that animus had nothing to do with the threat of global antisemitism. (Loeffler, p. 249) In the hands of Mali, Nigeria, and the United Arab Republic, who actually accused

Zionists of engineering the swastika epidemic, any talk of antisemitism was perversely reframed as a Zionist plot. The very word "Zionist" became a convenient and fungible term used by antisemites as a cover against charges of Jew hatred. Indeed, by the time the 1962 racism law was actually passed, the very law prompted by the swastikas, antisemitism was not even mentioned. A world turned upside down twice over. First, by its inability to understand Israel as anything other than some nefarious colonialist enterprise. And second, by its inability or unwillingness to differentiate between the safety of a vulnerable global Jewry and the deeds of Israel.

Truth be told, I had never heard of the swastika epidemic or the Year of Africa until I read Loeffler's book, but the third 1960 event I knew a bit about: the Eichmann trial. On May 23, 1960, Israel's Prime Minister David Ben-Gurion announced to the Knesset and the world that the Nazi war criminal Adolf Eichmann was under arrest in Israel and would stand trial. While we are familiar with the impact that announcement and subsequent trial had on the emotions of post-Holocaust Israeli and world Jewry – the transformation of a people from the persecuted to the prosecutor – this morning my focus is the reaction of the international community. *The Washington Post* scolded Israel's actions as "jungle law." Eichmann's capture and planned trial were deemed a mockery of justice, not to mention the international outrage that Argentina's sovereignty had been violated in his capture. Never mind that Eichmann had inflicted unspeakable crimes against the Jewish people, world opinion could not conscience a Jewish state with the power to seek justice for crimes committed against the Jews. Such hypocritical denouncements of Israel reached their ugly apotheosis with the image of a swastika embedded in a star of David in a satirical Soviet magazine. Zionism had become worse than Nazism, for whereas Nazi crimes occurred in some remote past, the Zionist outrage continued. In Loeffler's words "Zionism itself was on trial in the symbolic court of human rights." There is more to say. Loeffler's book is a must read, and, in case you are wondering, yes, I have already invited him to address our community. In simple terms, he relates the story of how three forces – the struggle against antisemitism, the recasting of Zionists as colonialist oppressors, and the world's inability to countenance a Jewish state who could and would stand up for itself – converged into a perfect and toxic storm that would pit Jews and the Jewish state in direct opposition to the progressive agenda. There was a time, lest we forget, when human rights and Zionism were seen as two sides of the same coin. It is no coincidence that in 1948 Jewish hands penned both Israel's Declaration of Independence and the Universal Declaration of Human Rights. But it was an alliance that would not last long. The events of 1960 became the backdrop for a world inhospitable to the proposition that Jews could lay claim to both the universal and particular, the progressive and parochial strands of their DNA.

It is now sixty years later, and it is tempting to think that the challenges on our campuses, in our high schools, and now even in our middle schools – of BDS, intersectionality, Britain's Labor Party, and otherwise – are new. It is tempting to lay blame for the Democratic party's increasingly lukewarm support for Israel on the toxic bromance between Trump and Netanyahu. No question, the Israeli and American administrations are not doing the world any favors lately, and anyone who knows me and my politics knows how horrified I am at the death of the two-state solution. But to think that somehow it is this or that policy of the Israeli government, or this or that peace plan proposed by the US administration that is the root of our present-day challenges, misses the longer arc of the story. The events of 1960 are significant because they demonstrate that the challenges of our day are neither new, nor the result of any one news cycle, leader, or annexation plan. It is important to think about 1960 because 1960 came before 1967: before the Six Day War, before the occupation of the West Bank, before Oslo, before Netanyahu, before Trump, before intersectionality, white privilege, before all these things. 1960 reflects a world which, like our own, tells Jews that, unlike any other people, they should not have the right to self-defense nor the right to self-determination, and that their expectation of either right only serves to reveal their unseemly and parochial privilege and national chauvinism.

This is what the world told the Jews in 1960; this is what the world is telling Jews today; and this is arguably what the world has been telling our people since our very founding as a nation, when we left Egypt as told in this week's Torah reading. Hundreds of years of servitude under the yoke of Pharaoh's oppression. The children of Israel crossing the sea from slavery to freedom. Finally, a tribe of our own, en route to the Promised Land, a place to call home. Yet scarcely had we crossed the sea, when along comes Amalek, attacking us, telling us that we were one tribe too many, that we should go back where we came from, to the place we had fled. Rabbinic tradition abounds in explanations of what Amalek represents: from the ancient antisemitic enemy of our people in the Torah, to Haman, to Hitler himself. This year, I ask you to consider that Amalek represents the pernicious and perennial claim that it is untoward for Jews to want the very things every person and every nation wants: safety and self-determination. Consider Amalek as the ugly and untrue allegation that for Jews to defend themselves is somehow in conflict with a commitment to building a just society. Amalek as the act of denying Jews the right to live in peace in their own sovereign homeland. It is the noxious contention that a Jew's right to a home is less valid than anyone else's. Amalek as a progressive world that prizes equity and inclusion for everyone – except Jews. A world that prizes diversity in just about everything – except opinion. A world eager to celebrate its liberalism except at the expense of its own unchallenged orthodoxies. Sometimes Amalek makes no bones about its intentions, attacking us openly on our journey, as in the Torah reading. Sometimes, as in 1960, Amalek disguises itself, cloaked in the language of anti-colonialism or human rights. Sometimes, like today, Amalek arrives in the form of the progressive vocabulary of intersectionality. It can come from our enemies, and yes, it can come from within our own ranks. It goes by different names, but it has been there since the very beginning, from generation to generation, the antisemitic claim that the only good Jew is a powerless Jew.

Some people say history repeats itself; others say that it rhymes. Interesting as that observation may be, far more interesting is how we respond to our present circumstances. As I stated a few weeks ago, I believe it is the obligation of Jews to stand strong and stand together in the face of anyone who would do harm to any member of our community no matter what kippah they wear or don't wear. I believe it is the obligation of all Jews to call out antisemitism as it comes from the right or the left, whether brazen or discreet, refusing to make allowance or alliance for either in the name of any short-term or injudicious gain. I believe that Zionism, the right of the Jewish people to a sovereign homeland, is a self-evident right and a Jewish obligation to defend. I believe that the nation-state of Israel, like all nation-states on this earth, is deeply imperfect and that my calling out its imperfections make me no less a Zionist than my criticisms of the United States make me any less a patriot. I believe that the fact that I believe myself to have journeyed from Egypt means that I have an obligation to my covenanted people and to the stranger in my midst and these obligations are part and parcel of my very being. I believe that these beliefs, self-evident as they are to me, are not so self-evident to all Jews (certainly not in the face of antisemites) and that it is the obligation of Jewish educational institutions, this one included, to position our youth to enter this world with the vocabulary, sophistication, and information they need to respond to the inhospitable thought communities that await them. Most of all, I believe it to be the obligation of every Jewish family to instill in their children a love of Judaism and love of Israel so that whatever it is their future holds, they will be proud and knowledgeable of who they are, of who their people are, of where they came from, and for what they are fighting.

Friends, our era does not lack for challenges. But for those with an eye for such things, in the broad arc of Jewish history, the decades in which our lives are playing out are as good as it gets. If it is to remain that way, if we are to ensure it remains the case for our children and grandchildren, we dare not sit complacent. There is work to be done; there are challenges to be addressed. No different than any generation, Amalek remains in our midst. Let us be vigilant, let us fight the good fight, and let us plant the seeds for our shared future.

February 8, 2020
13 Shevat 5780

Yitro
Standing at Sinai

Delivered at Sinai Temple in Los Angeles on the occasion of the second bar mitzvah of Rabbi Cosgrove's father, Dr. Malcolm Cosgrove

Of all the possible memories to retrieve at this moment, the one that strikes me as most relevant is my memory of the Cosgrove Shabbat table. The sound of the front door to our home opening and closing signaling my father's arrival from work, the beginning of Shabbat, and that our presence, without delay, was expected in the dining room. My mother would light the Shabbat candles; we would sing *Shalom Aleikhem*; my father would bless his four boys, my mother, and the wine. Before *hamotzi*, we washed hands – *n'tilat yadayim* – in silence, except, of course, for the yelp-inducing flicking of the hand towel on exposed skin, an act of fraternal aggression matched only by the scrum that would ensue over the prized middle piece of pull-apart challah. No matter the season – guests or no guests, dinner early or late – what came next never changed: Nobody could eat until mention was made of the weekly Torah portion. When we were little, it could be as brief as a check-in on our Hebrew reading skills. As we grew to be teenagers, our discussions became more robust, to include a range of medieval and contemporary commentaries. No parashah, no chicken soup – a childhood tradition that no doubt explains my Pavlovian affection for Torah. As the discussion wound down, my father would pose the closing question: "So, who thinks they know what the rabbi will talk about in shul tomorrow?" Would it be some aspect of the Torah reading, politics, the news out of Israel, or something else? Everyone took a guess. Shabbat morning arrived. We walked to shul. The Cosgrove family sat exactly where they are sitting today, and the rabbi began his sermon. Looks were passed, an eyebrow raised, victory declared by way of a silent fist pump or elbow to the ribs. Ben, Danny, Jason, my mother, or – more often than not – my father had gotten it right, had predicted the sermon topic, securing bragging rights until the cycle began again the following Shabbat.

Dad, *mazel tov* on your second bar mitzvah! Happy 83rd Birthday! Unlike the last time I spoke on this bimah – at my bar mitzvah, when you wrote my speech – today you have no idea what I am going to talk about!

All of us, I imagine, if given the opportunity, could retrieve a memory from our youth – a childhood experience, one-off or ongoing – that shapes who we are today. It could be a melody that reminds us of a place we once lived or a relationship we once were in. It could be the Proustian smell or taste of a food that prompts memories to burst forth. These memories make us who we are and connect us to others who share the same associations. The thrill I experience watching the Dodgers take the field at Chavez Ravine is not mine alone; it is a thrill I share with many others. It can be the books we read. The other day my son came home from school with a copy of *Catcher in the Rye* – a book I read when I was his age – starting an intergenerational conversation and connection by way of literature. Shared rituals, shared stories, shared memories – the ties that bind communities – are passed from one generation to another.

For me, "standing at Sinai" is a literal description. I step into this sanctuary and the floodgates of memory open. I know that the choices I have made, the life I have built, and the profession I have chosen can be traced back to Sinai. My love of the Jewish people, of Torah, of a good sermon, of beautiful music – these are present-day commitments seeded in this room and at my parents' Shabbat table long ago. But what for me is literal – a Jewish identity rooted at Sinai – is, according to tradition, the shared calling card for all Jews, no matter how or where we grew up. "Standing at Sinai" means that the events of this week's Torah reading – the receiving of Torah and the covenantal bond of our people – did not just happen in any one parashah, at any one time, or in any one place. "Standing at Sinai" means that you believe you heard God's voice and you perceive yourself, whether born Jewish or a Jew-by-choice, to be a stakeholder in an ongoing event of revelation and Jewish identity formation. No different than how the Passover Seder calls on us to affirm that we see ourselves as if we left Egypt, to be a Jew means that you see yourself as if you were standing at Sinai.

Mystical as the theology may be, it is not magical. Becoming a stakeholder at Sinai happens by means of a process of transmission from one generation to the next. The holidays we celebrate, the rituals we observe, the foods we eat, the books we read, the melodies we sing, even the tablecloths we use. Yes, some of these are *mitzvot*, commandments, but they are all vessels, vessels of transmission by which Jewish identity is passed on. As taught in *Pirkei Avot*, "The Ethics of Our Fathers," from Moses to Joshua, from Joshua to the elders, and so on and on until you and me. They constitute what the rabbis of old called *shalshelet ha-kabbalah*, the chain of tradition, the strands of Jewish DNA that reach back to Sinai. When it happens successfully – what sociologists describe as the mimetic transmission of Jewish practice – traditions are passed down one generation to the next. These vessels of identity are transformed from heirlooms of the past to proud trophies of the present. When the transmission is unsuccessful – when one generation finds itself unable, unwilling, or ill-equipped to take hold of the inheritance of prior generations, when one generation cannot hear, as it were, the voice of those who came before – the vessels become hollow and brittle, a rupture occurs, and the chain of tradition is severed.

For all the drama of this week's scene at Mount Sinai, I think the most intriguing exchange of the Torah reading is actually the one that comes at the start of the parashah – the arrival of Moses's father-in-law, Jethro, who, having heard the news of the Exodus, pays a visit to his son-in-law along with his daughter and grandsons. The eleventh-century commentator Rashi picks up on the psychological dimensions of Jethro's arrival by noting the ecstatic manner by which Moses greets his father-in-law – bowing down, kissing him – enthusiasm not lost on all who were present. Jethro was as close as Moses ever got to a father of his own. Lest we forget, the Torah offers no indication that Moses had any relationship with his biological father, Amram, perhaps explaining why Moses greeted Jethro so warmly. In fact, the Midrash explains that a few weeks ago, when Moses stood before the burning bush, God had to decide what voice to adopt. Too loud, and Moses might be frightened; too soft, and Moses might not listen. So God adopted the voice of Amram, Moses's father, to speak to him. (Exodus Rabbah 45:5) The most formidable obstacle Moses faced was not his stammering tongue; it was his lack of a connection to a father figure, or, to to put it another way, his inability to find his own voice a result of his not knowing the sound of his own father's voice. It certainly would explain why, in the wake of the golden calf, Moses pleads to see God's face, the face linked to the voice of his father. The self-doubt and insecurity that characterized Moses's ministry reflected his lifelong quest to hear his father's voice and see his father's face. There is rich Rabbinic debate as to why Jethro visited Moses and whether it was before or after Mount Sinai. Perhaps the best answer is the most simple: How could it be otherwise? Before Moses could receive the Law, his brokenness, his need for intergenerational connection, had to be addressed.

    I serve as rabbi to Park Avenue Synagogue, what people in this room refer to as the Sinai Temple of the East Coast. My rabbinate runs parallel to that of your rabbi, my colleague Rabbi David Wolpe. We share congregants, we visit the pope together, and it is one of the great blessings of my life that when faced with tough decisions, I do not just ask myself, "What would Rabbi Wolpe do?" I text or call my friend for advice. But beyond our friendship, beyond the fact that we share our pulpits with the two best cantors in America, we and the institutions we serve are all committed to retrieving for this generation the voice of prior generations, to rebuilding the severed link between Jewish generations, to guiding an American Jewry earnestly seeking to "stand at Sinai" but not quite sure how to get there. The experience my brothers and I shared at our parents' Shabbat table is not the shared experience of American Jewry. Most American Jews do not actually hear their father chant the Ten Commandments as I did this morning.

So how did we get where we are? It could be the rupture wrought by the Holocaust or the challenge of reconstituting an immigrant Jewish community in a new land. It could be the failure of Jewish education or the skyrocketing costs that keep it out of reach for so many. It could be the challenge of living in an open society, that seventy percent of non-Orthodox American Jews will marry someone not born Jewish, that you can do everything "right," and there is still no promise as to who your child will sit next to in freshman English. The fault could lie with the past; it could lie with the present. There is no shortage of explanations as to how we got where we are, no lack of finger pointing as to who is to blame. But far more constructive than complaining and blaming is asking what to do now. This is the project to which my synagogue, your synagogue, and all self-respecting synagogues are committed. How to inspire, enable, and empower an alienated American Jewry to lay claim to their rightful inheritance, to hear the voice of their fathers, and to stand proudly at Sinai.

But the synagogue cannot do it alone. Our children are reflections of the homes in which they grow up. You can stand on your soapbox and tell your kids to eat healthy, to be kind, and to live Jewishly. But your kids see you snacking late at night; they experience firsthand if you forgive freely; and they know better than anyone if you truly live Jewishly. You can fool some of the people all of the time, but you can't fool your kids for eighteen years. There are no promises in this world, but if you want your children to live Jewishly, it is you, not the rabbi or cantor, who will make the biggest difference. I, for one, know that if the Judaism of my own home is traditional and enlightened, reverential and warm, aspirational and humane, proud but not parochial, I need look no further than my parents' table to see how it happened. And on a day like today, it strikes me as both accurate and appropriate to reflect that if these qualities also infuse the community I lead, it is to the credit of the man who modeled them for me – my dad. Of all the possible expressions of the fifth commandment – *kaved at avikha v'et imekha*, Honor thy father and mother – perhaps the most obvious is the degree to which we make our parents' values evident, even when, if not especially when, they are not present.

I recall one Shabbat years ago, when I lived in Chicago, walking to synagogue with my daughter, then five years old, now on her way to college. As we walked hand-in-hand, I turned to her and said, "You know what, Lucy, here we are walking hand-in-hand to shul together and when I was a little boy, I walked to shul holding my daddy's, your grandpa's, hand. And you know what is even more fascinating, when grandpa was a little boy, he walked to shul holding his daddy's hand." On and on I went – confident that she had lost track and interest in what I found to be so fascinating – until the moment she paused, tugged at my hand, and responded with a question as pure as it was unexpected. She looked up at me and asked: "Daddy, did Moses walk to shul with his children?" I answered her the only way I knew how: "Yes, Lucy, Moses walked to shul with his children."

The path ahead is not an easy one. Challenges abound, the terrain is shifting, and the roadmap is not always clear. Let's at least commit to doing the one thing we can all do. Let's reach out our hand to the coming generation with the hope that they extend theirs in return. Let's lead by example, spending more time showing and less time telling. Step by step, hand-in-hand, generation to generation – until we are all standing together at Sinai.

February 15, 2020
20 Shevat 5780

The custom of a second bar/bat mitzvah is based on Psalm 90:10, which says that the human lifespan is 70 years. If age 70 is a new start, reaching age 83 is like becoming bnei mitzvah age again.

T'rumah
Let There Be Disruption

Fifty years ago today, at this precise moment, Rabbi Art Green began his dvar Torah based on the opening verses of this morning's parashah, *T'rumah*: "Speak to the children of Israel. Tell them to bring me gifts; take gifts for me from every person whose heart is so moved. Have them build for me a sanctuary that I may dwell among them." (Exodus 25:1-8)

A recent graduate of the Jewish Theological Seminary, Rabbi Green, together with about twenty other students and teachers, had created Havurat Shalom, a communal Jewish fellowship in Somerville, Massachusetts. The Havurah, as described by one of its founding members, Dr. David Roskies, was a combination ashram, monastery, *shtibl*, seminary, and urban kibbutz reflecting the counterculture of the late 1960s. While there was a practical element to the new seminary – it was a way for draft resisters to gain military deferments as ministry students – the driving ethos of this scrappy community was profound spiritual principles, both revolutionary and restorative.

They were revolutionary in that they rejected the establishment materialism of a 1950s "Goodbye Columbus" American Jewish life, rejected the frontal and formalized cantorial style of suburban synagogue prayer, rejected the dry scholasticism of existing rabbinical education, and rejected a host of social and political conventions received from prior generations. They were restorative in that unlike other radicals of the time who rejected religion altogether or turned to other faiths, the members of Havurat Shalom leaned into their

Judaism, seeking to retrieve the authentic spirit, sound, and teachings of Jewish tradition. They turned to contemplative hasidic prayer, to traditional Jewish study, and to a model of community membership based on a mutual covenant and dialogue, not on a membership form and check sent to a synagogue office. Whether it was beginning prayer services with wordless *niggunim*, participating in antiwar marches in DC, or concluding services by singing *Adon Olam* to "Scarborough Fair," Havurat Shalom represented a spiritual, scriptural, and communal retrieval of Judaism. Participants leveraged their unique spiritual gifts toward building a holy community. All of that was the gist of Rabbi Green's words that morning: how the private spiritual offerings of individuals could collectively serve to renew Judaism and build a home fit for God's presence.

The stories of Havurat Shalom and similar countercultural communities in New York, DC, and the Bay Area can be found in various histories of American Jewry, along with the nostalgia-or hallucinogen-tinged reminiscences of their founding members. This morning, I want to focus not so much on these communities, but on their reception, impact, and afterlife in American Judaism. At the time, Havurat Shalom was seen as a threat to the establishment. This week one of its founding members shared with me that when a local Boston rabbi confronted the Havurah saying that they should join the synagogue, they objected on the grounds that his pews were screwed (literally and figuratively) into the ground. And, truth be told, the heyday of Havurat Shalom did not last very long. Its utopian phase was just about five years. After the war, its founding members went on to build families and careers.

Yet despite its countercultural beginnings, despite its short-lived prime, fifty years later it is not an understatement to say that the spirit and members of Havurat Shalom have shaped American Jewry both directly and indirectly. Its impact can be measured in so many ways. There are scores of independent *minyanim* inspired by Havurat Shalom. Its founding personalities – Art Green, James Kugel, Michael Fishbane, and Michael Brooks, among others – constitute a generation of American Jewish spiritual, scholarly, academic, and institutional leadership. The do-it-yourself *Jewish Catalog* volumes found a place on countless bookshelves and opened the door to today's "how-to-do-Jewish" publications in print and online. Perhaps the greatest impact of these 1960s *havurot* is found in circumstances we live and breathe that are not easily catalogued or codified: women clergy; gender-neutral prayer language; American Jewry's present-day commitment to *tikkun olam*; the Melton, Meah, Limmud, and Study Circle classes that pervade Jewish communities, our own included; and the fact that one cannot participate in a prayer service without hearing a neo-hasidic melody, or in our case, *Halleluyah* sung to Leonard Cohen. The list goes on and on, but the point is one and the same. Havurat Shalom is important because it is a great case study for how disruptive innovation happens, in this case, within the American Jewish community. A new model that emerged in response to new circumstances and sentiments was initially overlooked or even rejected by the establishment, but eventually transformed from an ignored outsider to being integrated into the DNA of the very establishment against which it once rebelled.

Given the membership of this congregation, it is with great humility that I speak about anything to do with business or management theory. But ever since the sad and untimely passing of Harvard business professor Clayton Christensen last month, I have found myself totally intrigued by his theory of disruptive innovation, made famous in his celebrated 1997 book, *The Innovator's Dilemma*. Christensen describes what happens when an industry leader, focused on institutional stewardship and good management, proves unable to identify the new trends, circumstances, and opportunities on the horizon. As I understand the theory, a disruptive company emerges with an alternative and targets a segment of the market overlooked or underserved by its well-established competitors. Initially that alternative may be of inferior quality or only serve a narrow part of the market. Eventually, however, the disruptors get their act together and thus present a challenge to the industry leaders. Examples abound. RCA would not stop using vacuum tubes and was outfoxed by Sony and its transistors. Sears, once regarded as the best managed retailer in the world, failed to see the challenges of Walmart's lower pricing and Amazon's online shopping. Digital Equipment was blind to the arrival of desktop computers. Kodak lost its near monopoly in film with the emergence of digital photography. Most famously, Blockbuster Video was blindsided by Netflix, Hulu, and other streaming sites. Not every story leads to bankruptcy. There are some examples of accommodation, like the airlines that adapted to the challenge of JetBlue and Southwest, and Garmin, who refined their mission following the advent of Google Maps. The best example is probably Apple, with arguably the best second act in corporate history. Having introduced the first personal computers in 1976, it was then nearly completely overrun by Microsoft's operating system, but then went on to totally reinvent itself with iPods, iTunes, iPhone, iPads, and the rest is history. The success stories are those companies who are eyes wide open to the emerging landscape, learn from the disruptors, integrate what they have learned into their own model, and boldly reconstruct their missions toward meeting, or even defining, the future.

Christensen, God-fearing Mormon he was, knew his Bible, so I imagine he would have appreciated the example of disruptive innovation in this week's Torah reading. The children of Israel, having just received the law at Mount Sinai, had to transform their communal structure, national identity, and religious life from the base of Mount Sinai to the wilderness wandering ahead. Remaining at the mountain was not an option; there was an obligation to seek the Promised Land. But leaving the site of revelation risked taking leave of the divine presence. The thirteenth century Spanish commentator Nahmanides suggests that it is precisely this dilemma that prompted the innovation of the Mishkan, the desert tabernacle that would accompany the Israelites in the years ahead. The centralized model of Sinai had served its purpose; the *Shekhinah*, God's presence, would no longer abide solely at the mountaintop. The Mishkan became the portable transistor, if you will, enabling Moses and all of Israel to experience God's presence wherever they wandered. The pattern is there: a challenge to the received model; an innovation introduced; and the religion of Israel is revolutionized and sustained from one chapter to the next. It is not a complete triumph: there will be setbacks, including the sin of the golden calf just around the corner. But for the moment, it a model of reconstruction that would make any MBA proud.

This spirit – this spirit of reconstructing the model of our faith – has been the hallmark of our people's strength from generation to generation. The Mishkan would not last forever. When Israel arrived in the Promised Land, they once again turned to a centralized model, experiencing God's presence in the Jerusalem Temple. When the Temple was destroyed at the hands of the Romans, the innovations of the Pharisees transformed Judaism from a Temple-based faith to a Rabbinic religion. The Shabbat table is known as a *mikdash m'at* – a Temple in miniature – where we experience God's presence in our homes every week. Sometimes the transformation is willing; sometimes it is a response to catastrophe. Sometimes the establishment embraces the disruptive innovator, and sometimes it resists. The story of Havurat Shalom fifty years ago is instructive because it represents an example of disruptive innovation that, in retrospect, served to bolster the establishment Jewish community. It is yet another case when our people, faced with new conditions, undertook to re-express our inheritance, integrating the new with the old, so that today we cannot imagine Jewish life otherwise.

And in case you are wondering, it is this sentiment that is informing the present efforts of this community. As you may know, having completed the dedication of our new campus, we are embarking on a strategic plan to set the course for our future. We are asking questions about worship, programming, social justice, congregational school, travel education, inclusion – about just about everything. But more important than addressing any particular sphere of synagogue life is the spirit guiding our efforts. What are we not doing that we need to do? What are others doing that we need to do better? What are the trends on the horizon that we need to be alert and responsive to? Who are the disruptors in our midst and how can we integrate their wisdom into our present efforts? If 70 percent of Jews will marry someone not born Jewish, how shall we position the synagogue for this reality? In a world where support for Israel has been politicized to a toxic degree, how can the synagogue help bridge the divide? As we bask in the beauty of our revitalized building and affirm our strength, can we identify the seen and unseen barriers preventing others from accessing the richness of Jewish life?

This is not about a change of mission. As long as I am here, this synagogue will remain true to being a house of prayer, of study, and of community – a place to inspire, educate, and support our membership towards living passion-filled Jewish lives. But in order to stay vital so that we can accomplish that mission, we must remain self-reflective, willing to be called out on our blind spots, and willing to learn from others. We are not Blockbuster, nor are we Apple. We are an industry leader with a self-imposed insistence on constantly reimagining what we do. As the late Andy Grove remarked: "Success breeds complacency. Complacency breeds failure. Only the paranoid survive." There are those in this world who would have you believe that the game is won by sticking to the fundamentals of blocking and tackling, and there are others who chase innovation and trick plays. We reject that choice as false. In the words of my favorite industry leader, the late, great Bo Schembechler, in this Big House we emphasize both execution *and* innovation, loyal to our principles and ready to scrap the script if a new one is needed.

"Build for me a sanctuary that I may dwell among them." Fifty years ago, five hundred years ago, thousands of years ago – our people's call to action has always been to build a communal vision fit to house God's presence. That mission is as compelling as when it was first stated. We know that. Our eyes, hearts and minds must always remain open to how we accomplish it, the materials we use, the people we learn from. Each of us has the gift of ourselves to give towards the project. I invite you to be part of the process and help to build our very bright collective future.

February 29, 2020
4 Adar 5780

Further Reading:

Christensen, Clayton. *The Innovator's Dilemma*, New York: Harper Business, 1997; reprint edition, Harvard Business Review Press, 2016 (e-book at the New York Public Library)

Oppenheimer, Mark, *Knocking on Heaven's Door: American Religion in the Age of Counterculture* (New Haven: Yale University Press, 2003) (in the PAS Library)

Roskies, David G., "A Jewish World of Infinite Possibility: Looking Back at 50 Years of Havurat Shalom," *Tablet*, May 24, 2018
    https://www.tabletmag.com/jewish-life-and-religion/261461/havurat-shalom-at-50

T'tzavveh/Shabbat Zakhor
Purim in the Time of Coronavirus

Writing a sermon without knowing whether I will actually deliver it is something I have never done – until this week. Over the past week, we have all been thrust into unprecedented territory. The outbreak of the novel coronavirus here in New York City has transformed what had been an overseas abstraction into an immediate and imminent concern. First and foremost, our thoughts and prayers go out to all those individuals and families who are ill, as we pray for their comfort, healing, and recovery. We have all been impacted – in our workplaces, in our schools, and in our homes. We are sorting fact from fiction and healthcare expertise from hysteria as our world has been turned upside down in ways I have never experienced in my lifetime. We are checking in with our elderly parents; we are concerned for the well-being of our children away at college or on travel education programs; and we are calculating risk vs. reward for the simple act of dropping off our children at school.

The Hebrew word for a synagogue is *beit knesset* – "a house of gathering" – a place for people to come together at set times on the Jewish calendar and in the lifecycle. How exactly should a *beit knesset* respond in a moment of social distancing, where people are giving elbow bumps, not handshakes, hellos but no hugs, where people can't come to minyan to say kaddish? In the next two days we will have our Purim celebration, an annual communal happening complete with a long-rehearsed Purim spiel, children's costume parades and carb-rich hamentashen. Do we still have the carnival? Some say yes, others no. Some say yes, but no bouncy castle and no face painter and no ring toss. And then someone asks: "At what point does a carnival stop being a carnival?" These are real conversations, in real meetings, which I have been part of this week. And beneath it all lurks the very real anxiety that nobody knows what is to come in the days or even hours ahead. Every conversation is shot through with contingency, every meeting with an implicit "in the event of." We are in a haphazard and happenstance world whose only operating principle seems to be chance, a world where rabbis don't even know if the sermons they write will be delivered in shul on Shabbat.

Like a royal diadem that shines brightly in every direction, there is no shortage of ways to appreciate the scroll of Esther we will read on Monday night. We can read it as a feminist story about its namesake, Esther – a twice marginalized Jewish woman who negotiates her way through a patriarchy to lead her people in their hour of need. Alternatively, Esther is a political tale describing a vulnerable Jewish people, an account of how the Jews of Shushan negotiate power as a minority diaspora community. Or you can read Esther as a treatise on the dynamics of antisemitism, how in every generation there arises a Haman-like figure filled with maniacal hatred against our people. Another reading, of course, is that Esther is a Disneyesque or even burlesque satire, with kings and beauty queens, heroes and villains, royal feasts and quiet courage. The Hebrew Bible, after all, is not a single book but a library, and every library should contain at least one fairy tale.

There are many ways to appreciate the story of Esther, but this year I want to choose an obvious one suggested by the very name Purim, and that is "chance." The story is one twist after the other, a series of coincidences, unplanned encounters, and reversals of fortune. Let's start at the very beginning. What if King Ahasuerus had not called on Vashti to appear? What if Vashti had not refused, thus not leaving the throne open for a new queen? What if Mordechai, Esther's cousin, had not been in the right place at the right time to overhear the plot to assassinate the King? What are the odds that when the sleepless king asked that the book of records be brought to him, his servants would read just the passage about Mordechai's loyalty? And what is the likelihood that just that night, Haman would happen to be waiting in the courtyard? The list goes on. Again and again the driver of this story will be serendipity. No question, all these reversals serve the literary purpose of keeping readers young and old engaged in the story. But the message runs deeper. After all, the name of the holiday is not Esther Day, Diaspora Day, or Jewish V-Day. The name of the holiday is "Purim" – from the word *pur*, meaning "lot" – the process by which Haman chose the date of our destruction. It was a lottery, the very symbol of a world governed by chance. According to tradition, the guiding principle of the story is the upending of expectations: *v'nahafokh hu*. (Esther 9:1) The story of Esther is many things, but at its core, it reminds us that none of us is as in control of our lives as we would like to believe. Unlike the book of Deuteronomy, which teaches that good is rewarded with good and bad with bad, or Ecclesiastes, which teaches that there is a right time, *eit*, for everything, for this one day of the year, there is one book of the Bible that says maybe, just maybe, it ain't so. Despite what we may wish and perhaps even believe about providential design, maybe it is chance, luck, or, in Hebrew, *mazal* that has the first and final word in the tale of our lives.

And if it is indeed the case that the whole point of the Esther story is that life is a lottery and that none of us knows what will happen from one moment to the next, then that realization is also the lens that snaps the redemptive message of the holiday into focus. We know the scene well: The fate of the Jews has been sealed by wicked Haman, and Mordechai makes a last-ditch effort to contact his cousin Esther, who is comfortably ensconced in her royal surroundings. As did Moses, as did other leaders before her, when called on to lead, Esther demurs, fearing the risks, filled by self-doubt. "You've got the wrong princess, Mordecai. I am only allowed to approach the King at certain times, in certain circumstances." It is at this point that Mordechai implores her: "Do not imagine to yourself that in the King's house you will escape from among all your people. *U-mi yodea im l'eit ka-zot higaat l'malkhut.* Who knows whether for a moment just like this you arose to power." (4:14) The Hebrew is important. It was not until this year that I realized that the key phrase *l'eit ka-zot*, "a moment just like this" contains the same word that Ecclesiastes uses when speaking of the moments of our lives: *eit la-ledet, v'eit la-mut*, "a time to be born, a time to die." It is almost as if, if not exactly as if, Mordechai is saying to his cousin: "Look Esther, none of us really knows how we got here and none of us is in control of what tomorrow brings. The only thing we can control in this world turned upside-down is whether and how we choose to respond to the unplanned. We can respond with courage, with wisdom, with the well-being of our people in mind, or we can abdicate human agency. Who knows what will happen one moment, one *eit*, to the next? What we do know, what is in your power is our response to moments just like this. Nobody has a crystal ball, but we can turn anxiety into confidence, fear into poise, and inattention to responsibility." It is at this point that Esther herself is transformed, literally coming out from hiding (which is what "Esther" actually means in Hebrew) emboldened and empowered. The story does not end there. There are challenges and reversals yet to come; we are only in chapter four of a ten-chapter tale. But it is here that Esther takes on heroic stature, leaning in to shape her people's destiny.

To this day, the four mitzvot associated with Purim speak to this very ethic of Esther.

- First: hearing the megillah read. No different than the Passover Seder, as Mordechai told Esther that fateful night, one must see oneself as a participant in the story of our people. You have to hear the megillah read.

- *Second: Matanot la'evyonim, gifts to the poor.* According to Jewish law, you must give to at least two people at least enough for a minimal meal, even if you yourself have limited resources. Why? No doubt because giving gifts to the poor reminds us of human agency. It reminds us that if we are sitting in this room, as Esther did in hers, whatever our worries may be, our worries are the kind most people would love to have. We are all very, very lucky, we should never forget our good fortune, and we should always give to those to whom fate has not been as kind.

- *Third, and this is my favorite: Mishloach Manot, or in Yiddish, Shaloch Manos.* Everyone is obligated to send a gift of food – usually a tasty, high-calorie treat – to another person, a gesture of kindness, friendship, and community building.

- *Fourth and finally, the seudah, the festive meal.* Like the *mishloach manot*, the festive meal is a reminder of the importance of fellowship, community, and maybe, too, of keeping good humor in times of uncertainty.

Practically speaking, I do hope to fulfill all four mitzvot this week, and I hope you do as well. For all I know, we may be hearing the megillah read via livestream. But find a way to observe the mitzvot of Purim in some way because they remind us that even, if not especially, during those moments when the ground is shifting beneath us, we are not powerless. We are part of a bigger story and we can all move the needle ever so slightly in our own lives and the lives of those around us. We can all go online and bring a smile to someone's face by sending them an unexpected treat. We can reach into our pocket and help someone perform the most basic act of feeding themselves. If Purim is the day of the year meant to remind us that we are in less control that we think we are, the mitzvot of Purim are the prompts meant to stir us to action, so that like Esther, with wisdom and quiet courage, we try our best to shape the world around us.

I began writing this sermon not knowing if it would be delivered. And now that it has been delivered, I can't tell you what will happen between now and the end of Shabbat. But I do know that when Shabbat ends, this week and every week, when I make Havdalah, I will recite the words from the book Esther, *La-y'hudim hayitah orah v'sim ḥah v'sasson vikar,* that we "should enjoy light and gladness, joy and honor." (8:16) In other words, the tradition is teaching that if we stop and think about it, if we really stop to think about it, the uncertainty of this week isn't limited to just this week. Life can always be turned on its head; none of us really knows what any one moment will bring. And yet we can respond to those moments, as Esther did in her time of darkness, by taking agency, leaning in, keeping our wits and sense of humor, and most of all, by writing ourselves into the story, giving of our humanity and our blessings, turning anxiety to confidence, grief to joy, and darkness to light, gladness, joy and honor.

March 7, 2020
11 Adar 5780

Va-yikra
The Next Right Thing

Even rabbis, lest you think otherwise, turn to rabbis for support. And if there was ever a week that rabbis were in need of support, counsel, and guidance, this past week was the one. Through the good services of the New York Board of Rabbis, the other day I participated in a clergy-only Zoom meeting to speak openly about the challenges my colleagues and I were facing as we tended to the pastoral needs of our respective communities.

Not everyone on the call was a congregational rabbi. There were teachers, educators, chaplains, and administrators; their stories varied depending on the community served. One rabbi, the chaplain to Rikers Island jail, described the weighty choices being made in our correctional facilities as to whether to keep inmates in isolation or to allow them to interact with other inmates and risk exposure. Another rabbi, the chief chaplain in a local psychiatric facility, described the isolation of the patients and the debates taking place as to whether or not clergy and mental health professionals should provide psychosocial support in this time of social distancing – a damned if you do, damned if you don't choice. My congregational colleagues shared stories of couples deciding whether to postpone a wedding, families seeking counsel as to whether to reschedule long-planned bnei mitzvah, or if it is preferred to have a circumcision right away in the hospital or wait until the eighth day and risk exposure. One colleague told of a particularly acrimonious divorce in his community, in which the civil settlement between the parties required that the *get*, the Jewish divorce document, be executed within a certain time frame, a time frame now rendered impossible, because in order to execute a *get*, you must have multiple witnesses in the same room.

In every instance, my colleagues were being asked what should be done. So many individual stories, not to mention real-time management decisions to stay open or not, to hold services or not, to make budget or staff freezes or not. Our problems varied, but our state of mind was alike. So many decisions, each one of great consequence, each one with multiple stakeholders holding different opinions, each one needing to be made on the spot – a firehose of decisions showing no sign of letting up. We were all worn down, we were all fatigued. I am not sure if the call solved anything, but it was certainly therapeutic, if for no other reason, than to know that the pressures I faced in my rabbinate this past week were not unique to me. Decision fatigue is a burden I do not shoulder alone.

This morning I want to speak to you about the COVID-19 pandemic not as a health care professional; my expertise is no more or less than any other non-medical professional. I want to speak from the perspective of a pastor and reflect on but one of the many effects this public health crisis is having on all of our psyches, individually and collectively.

I recently read an article by John Tierney about a study conducted by two Israeli researchers, Jonathan Leva of Stanford and Shai Danziger of Ben-Gurion University, entitled "Extraneous Factors in Judicial Decisions." To make a long article short, the researchers evaluated the decisions made by a parole board in the Israeli prison system. What Leva and Danziger discovered was that whether a prisoner was paroled or not had nothing to do with the prisoner's ethnic background, the crimes they had committed, or the sentences they had received. After analyzing over 1,100 decisions over the course of a year, they discovered that the greatest predictor in outcome was the time of day in which the parole board heard the case. Prisoners who appeared early in the morning were paroled seventy percent of the time; those who appeared late in the day, less than ten percent of the time. If your case was heard just before lunch, your odds were far worse than after lunch. The paper received quite a bit of press at the time. On the one hand, it revealed the disquieting truth that the dispensation of justice can be contingent on levels of rest or glucose, but it was also affirming, in that it documented something about the human condition that we all know intuitively to be true, namely, that our ability to make decisions is like a muscle. And that decision-making muscle, like any muscle, can become fatigued, can become strained, can give out on us, which is why we need to treat it well, with care, with rest, and with caution.

As I read about decision fatigue, I began to think of an endless number of examples, in my life and all around, that supported the idea. I thought of a doctoral advisor of mine about whom I realized after my first semester in graduate school that I should only speak to him in the first half of the day, because I could ask him the same question in the morning and in the afternoon, and no different than the Israeli judges, he would give me a totally different answer. I think of my father, who once shared with me that he far prefers speaking to me on Sunday night when the pressures of Shabbat are behind me, than on Thursday night when I am frantically trying to finish my sermon. I think of Moses, who while leading the Israelites through the desert, was reprimanded by his father-in-law Jethro for seeking to adjudicate all the cases brought before him. "What you are doing is not right, you will wear yourself out," Jethro tells Moses. It wasn't right for Moses and it wasn't right for Israel who risked being led by a leader unable to call balls and strikes. What if, I wondered, decision fatigue is a psychological explanation of the riddle of Pharaoh's hardened heart? To let Israel go would be to capitulate to Moses; to keep the Israelites enslaved would be to endure more plagues – a dilemma that would paralyze anyone, even a Pharaoh.

Decision fatigue explains why, in taxonomy of sacrifices in this week's Torah reading, there is an entire chapter on the various offerings for intentional and unintentional sins. Leviticus was well aware that nobody goes very far in life without a misstep in judgment. No doubt decision fatigue was behind Adam and Eve's ill-fated choice to eat of the fruit of the garden. Decision fatigue is behind every ill-advised decision made after 2:00 am since the beginning of time. As my physician once told me, it is not the calories in the wine you drink that are the problem, it is the calories of the ice cream you consume after you have the wine, after your judgment is impaired, that are the problem. The effects of decision fatigue are everywhere in our lives: the effects of the mental exhaustion wrought by the task of making decisions – weighing the pluses and minuses of any course of action and having to make an imperfect choice in a short time – the consequences of which both we and others will have to live with.

It is that feeling, on steroids, which is how I believe we all feel right now. I can only speak to the pressures of being a rabbi; I cannot claim to speak with authority about other fields and walks of life. But I have spent much of the week hearing the stories of many members of the community. It is always hard in the business world to juggle the variables that go into management decisions, but those variables have now multiplied and turned erratic and rapid in ways members of our community have not seen in their lifetimes. Not just whether to buy or sell, but how to maintain a company remotely. How to treat employees when retirement plans have been materially impaired, and the looming question of when a management team deems it safe or unsafe to reopen – weighing the relative risks of lost business versus employee health. What about the medical professionals debating the allocation of precious resources, including the most precious resource of all – themselves – towards patient care? At what point should someone be admitted to the hospital, be intubated or not? What about in our personal lives? Go to work or stay home? See a parent or friend in need, if doing so puts us at personal risk? Give birth without a partner present or give birth outside a hospital system where a partner can be present, but the mother could be at risk if there's a complication? And so on and on and on. Financial professionals, medical professionals, educators, delivery men, and doormen – there is system overload for everyone, especially when we are working full speed 24/7 with no end in sight.

How I wish, more than you know, that I had the answer – that this would be the part of the sermon where I untie the knot and explain how we should all move forward. But I don't have the answer. All I can do, the best I can do, at least what I am trying to do – as in my call earlier in the week with my colleagues – is to give voice to some of my anxieties, which may be some of your anxieties, which may just help us all realize that we are not as alone as we may think we are. And perhaps, if we all allow for the fact that each one of us, in our respective lanes, is just doing our level best to make the wisest decisions we can, based on the limited information and limited time we have – well, maybe we will all be that much more patient, more forgiving, more communicative, and more trusting of ourselves and of others. None of us can do it alone; we all need to have confidence that our colleagues and friends are operating with the best of intentions; and we can't relitigate their judgment at the very moment that a cascade of new decisions are waiting to be made. It is not easy in the present environment, but we need to find ways to let that decision-making muscle rest and replenish – through sleep, with exercise, by whatever means possible – so that we will make the next decision we are asked to make with as sound judgment as possible

These last weeks have taught me much; most of all, they have taught me how little I know and how little we all know about the future. But I am getting the sense that this sprint is turning into a marathon, or, more likely, a marathon at the pace of a sprint. And if that is the case, and if we intend to see this through, then we must build up the necessary emotional reserves and spiritual resources to go the distance. To mix my metaphors, we all need to acknowledge that in this fight we are all punching way above our weight. None of us holds the answers. So let's work together, with humility, with courage, with trust, and with confidence, seeking to do the next right thing, and then the next and then the next, until one day, please God, we will look back at this time saying it too has passed – a string of imperfect decisions that led us out of the wilderness and back to the perfectly imperfect lives to which we so long to return.

March 28, 2020
3 Nisan 5780

Tierney, John, "Do You Suffer from Decision Fatigue?" *The New York Times Magazine*, August 21, 2011
https://www.nytimes.com/2011/08/21/magazine/do-you-suffer-from-decision-fatigue.html

Pesaḥ, 2nd Day
The Question of Suffering

This spring marks the seventieth anniversary of the passing of one of my distinguished predecessors at Park Avenue Synagogue: Rabbi Milton Steinberg. Rabbi Steinberg, who tragically died of a heart attack at the age of 46 in March 1950, served Park Avenue from 1933 to 1950 and was the founding rabbi of Park Avenue in its "modern era." Under his dynamic leadership the synagogue experienced tremendous growth, transforming into a leading congregation in North America. In addition to his congregational profile, Rabbi Steinberg was one of the chief ideologues of Reconstructionist Judaism and the righthand man to its founder, Rabbi Mordecai Kaplan. Rabbi Steinberg was also a prolific author and theologian in his own right. To this day, his books *As A Driven Leaf* and *Basic Judaism* among others have their place on countless Jewish bookshelves.

Given the impossibility of summarizing Rabbi Steinberg's rabbinate – his pastoral presence, his felicitous pen, his leadership qualities – today I would like to examine his legacy by way of one sermon, a Passover sermon he delivered sometime in the 1940s, which has been preserved in outline form in a volume compiled by Bernard Mandelbaum.

The sermon is ostensibly about the fourth child of the Passover Haggadah, a child whom we have read about these past two evenings, the *she'eino yodea lish'ol*, the one who, unlike his siblings, does not even know how to ask a question. The beginning of the sermon is straightforward enough, but in exploring the meaning of this enigmatic fourth child, Steinberg goes on to cite another sermon, this one delivered by Rabbi Levi Yitzhak of Berdichev (1740–1810), the saintly figure of 18th-century Hasidism, a man who knew personal suffering – the loss of a child – as well as the travails experienced by his people. For all of his many qualities, Rabbi Levi Yitzhak is remembered as one of the great defenders of the Jewish people, willing to bring God to account for the suffering of God's people.

"The Haggadah speaks of four sons," Rabbi Levi Yitzhak explains, "one wise, one wicked, one simple, and one who does not know how to ask. Lord of the world, I, Levi Yitzhak, am the one who does not know how to ask. Lord of the universe, even if I did know, I would not dare to [ask]. How could I venture to ask You [God] why everything happens as it does, why we suffer, why we are driven from one exile to another, why our foes are allowed to torment us?" Rabbi Levi Yitzhak continued in his cry to God, "But the Haggadah explains to the father of this fourth child: The father must take the initiative. Lord of the world, are You not my Father? Am I not Your son? I do not even know what questions to ask. I do not beg You to reveal to me the secret of your ways – I couldn't comprehend it! But please show me one thing. Show me the meaning of what is happening to me at this moment. Show me what it demands of me. Show me what You, Lord of the universe, are telling me through it. I do not ask why I suffer. I ask only to know that I suffer for your sake."

I ask only to know that I suffer for your sake.

It is a terse pain-filled homily, a message preached by Rabbi Levi Yitzhak in Berdichev some two and a half centuries ago in the midst of exile and torment and delivered again by Rabbi Steinberg on the Upper East Side in the 1940s. The question of the fourth child is notable both for its remarkable concession and its insistent demand on God. On the one hand, "I do not ask why I suffer." On the other hand, "I ask to know only that I suffer for your sake." Levi Yitzhak knows the inevitability of pain; he knows the life of quiet desperation that most people lead; he accepts pain as an unwelcome but necessary part of the human experience. Levi Yitzhak is theologically modest enough not to ask why suffering exists. Nevertheless he makes a demand of God. He wants to know is if there is a bigger purpose to his suffering. In secular terms: "Is there something good to come of it?"

And I think it is perhaps this same question that motivated Steinberg that Passover morning. Steinberg's intellectual interests touched on the full range of Jewish study and concern, but when this sermon was written, in his final few years, at the peak of his intellectual prowess, as he led our community through the shadows of the Shoah, not to mention his own failing health, Steinberg stood face-to-face with what his student (and product of this congregation) Arthur Cohen called "the Tremendum," the unspeakable theological questions raised by the Shoah. Steinberg had to contend with the overwhelming thought of a God under whose watch the Holocaust took place. Given his national profile, Steinberg was on the front lines of the American Jewish speaking circuit, mobilizing American Jewry to provide relief to refugees, raising funds on their behalf, building up the fledgling state of Israel, and most difficult of all, trying to make sense of the Shoah to a Jewry in search of meaning.

To give you one of many examples, I share with you a passage from what I believe to be one of Rabbi Steinberg's most heart-searing addresses, "When I Think of Seraye." Speaking in 1944 to the Women's Division of the United Jewish Appeal at the Waldorf Astoria, Steinberg describes Seraye, "a village situated in the Lithuanian County of Suwalki, just to the east of the old German frontier." A village, in Steinberg's words "whence my family stems, where my father was born." "I say," writes Steinberg, "that I have been thinking about Seraye a great deal of late [because] I cannot think about all of Europe's Jews, the six million dead, the one and a half million walking skeletons. Such numbers are too large for me to embrace, the anguish they represent is too vast for my comprehension. And so, I think of Seraye instead." Steinberg recounts imagined people and scenes of this village that is no longer, and by extension, the countless Serayes destroyed by the Nazis. He is filled with anguish and anger. "Sometimes," he writes, "when I think of Seraye, I want to hurl hard words at God, that terrible saying of Abraham; 'Shall the Judge of the whole earth not do Justice?!'"

Again and again, in speech after speech, Steinberg would seek to formulate a response to the sufferings of humanity. Again, in his own words: "The hard tragic fact is that of the universality of suffering, the truth that to live is to suffer. . . . All life is a great fellowship of anguish in which each of us participates in some fashion or other." Steinberg's questions were the same questions as those of Levi Yitzhak, the unspoken theological question of the fourth child, "Not why is there suffering, but for what purpose is this suffering?"

And on that Passover morning in the 1940s, Steinberg continued to explain his view: There is all the difference in the world between pain that leads to something and pain that leads to nowhere . . . the former is more bearable, may even be welcomed. The pain experienced by a woman giving birth. The compromises in health one endures in order to battle cancer or the sacrifices, anxieties, strains, and tensions one accepts if serving a greater good. It is not pain that is intolerable, but pain that is senseless. If one could be sure that their suffering is for God's sake, what a difference that would make not only in the midst of a particular ordeal – but in all of life – since life and pain are interwoven.

What Steinberg is saying, what Levi Yitzhak is saying is that if a person is able to determine that their ordeal will have meaning, that is what makes all the difference. Here we are today, a suffering humanity, the terms of our suffering different than that of Levi Yitzhak's time, different than that of Steinberg's time, but suffering all the same. And here we are – again the fourth child – wondering if there is meaning to our suffering.

And the truth is that I don't know. There are people fighting for their lives, there are people dying. There are people without work, without family, without the means to feed themselves. In thinking of the lives upended at this moment, I can only adopt the language of Steinberg: The numbers are too large for me to embrace; the anguish they represent is too vast for my comprehension. Is there meaning to present suffering? It strikes me as premature and untoward and unseemly to have the audacity to assign meaning to the sufferings of our hour as we stand in the eye of the storm of this terrible plague.

Lacking an answer, I will instead offer Steinberg's words that day in the midst of the darkness of the 1940s. Steinberg explains that in life, every person always has an audience of at least two. For the theologically minded, the two are God and the person him- or herself. Those without a belief in God still have the audience of themselves. Every person, when faced with suffering, has a choice of how to respond.

If, Steinberg writes, suffering turns a person cruel, selfish, and bitter – then that response is a reflection not only of themselves, not only of humanity, but also of God. If, on the other hand, a person's suffering turns them merciful, kind, and compassionate – if a person carries their suffering with dignity – then that response is also a demonstration not only of the individual's spirit, not only of humanity's essential nobility, but also, ultimately, of God's glory.

Suffer you will, concludes Steinberg, that is your lot. Fret not to understand why – there is no answer to the question, nor would you understand it if it were disclosed to you. Concern yourself, rather, only with this: That your sufferings shall be for God's sake – a task accomplished by enhancing the dignity of humanity, by extending patience, compassion, care, empathy, and benevolence to your loved ones, to yourself, and to the masses of humanity in crying need of compassion and kindness. When you do so, humanity will be elevated in the eyes of all who look upon you – in God's eyes, if you believe in God, but at the very least, in your own.

Friends, I have no idea why humanity suffers. Neither did Rabbi Steinberg, Rabbi Levi Yitzhak, or anyone else. I only know, as did they, that whether there is purpose to our suffering is a question that is ultimately not up to God, but to each one of us.

May the memory of Rabbi Milton Steinberg, *HaRav Micha'el ben Shmuel HaLevi*, be for a blessing, and may we all respond to our present tribulations by making every effort to enoble our lives and the lives of others, thus granting meaning to our suffering.

April 10, 2020
16 Nisan 5780

Shabbat Hol Ha-moed Pesaḥ
Social Solidarity . . . Not Distancing

Despite the fact that Debbie and I lived in Chicago for ten years beginning in the late 1990s, it was not until this week that I heard of the 1995 Chicago Heat Wave. As Dr. Eric Klinenberg describes in *Heat Wave: A Social Autopsy of Disaster in Chicago*, on the first day of the heat wave, Thursday, July 13, 1995, the temperature hit 106 degrees, which in combination with the humidity, felt like 120 degrees to Chicagoans. That week, roads buckled, train rails warped, and children riding in school buses became so dehydrated they had to be hosed down by the Fire Department. Energy usage went sky-high, leading to a failure of power grids, and so many fire hydrants were opened that some neighborhoods lost not only electricity but also water. The emergency crews that came to seal hydrants were greeted by overheated citizens throwing bricks and rocks to keep them away. Paramedics couldn't keep up with emergency calls, and city hospitals were overwhelmed. Some ambulance crews drove around the city for miles looking for an open bed. By Saturday, just three days later, capacity at the morgue was exceeded by hundreds; a fleet of refrigerated trucks had to be brought in to store the bodies. The "excess death" rate, Klinenberg recounts – meaning the difference between the number of fatalities that week as compared to a typical week – was 739. That is, 739 Chicago residents suffered heat-related deaths.

Government response was both insufficient and tone-deaf, with Mayor Richard M. Daley advising, "Let's not blow it out of proportion. . . . Every day people die of natural causes. You cannot claim that everybody who has died in the last eight or nine days dies [sic] of heat." If you, like I, have never heard of that heat wave, part of the reason may be the legacy of Mayor Daley's callous skepticism. By the end of the summer even Chicagoans debated whether the heat deaths were "really real." ("Dying Alone," Interview with Eric Klinenberg, University of Chicago Press, 2002)

Klinenberg's credentials, however, are not in meteorology or public health. He is a sociologist and his study of the heat wave revealed that it was not just a natural disaster but a social disaster as well. The mortality rates did not impact men and women equally, did not impact rich and poor equally, did not impact white, black, and Latino equally. Most interestingly, Klinenberg explains, the disparate mortality rates can be tracked not just by ethnic or economic divides, but by the degree of social cohesion within communities. The tight-knit communities, where people checked in on each other, enjoyed strong family ties, shared public space and social services – those communities weathered the heat wave more successfully, and fewer people died. But in neighborhoods where residents were out of contact with family and friends and unassisted by public agencies or community groups, it was in those communities where residents – seniors and otherwise – died alone, often behind closed doors and sealed windows. Drawing on the language of Emile Durkheim, one of the founding figures of sociology, Klinenberg points to the importance of "organic solidarity," the idea that we are all interdependent. It is the key variable to survival – not just in the Chicago heat wave, but in Hurricane Katrina, Hurricane Sandy, and other natural disasters. Yes, these calamities reflected nature's fury, not to mention systemic failures of government, but the extent to which they were disastrous correlated with the presence or absence of social trust and cohesion. These calamities were plagues that were not distributed evenly, their effects were experienced differently by different communities – differences that made all the difference in the world when it came to the most important difference: life or death.

Last week, in preparing for all my Zoom seders, or "Zeders" as my children call them, for obvious reasons, I found myself, like many of us, absorbed by the Ten Plagues. Why did God send the plagues? Why ten? Why these ones in particular? Why in this particular order? Why did God harden Pharaoh's heart with each successive plague? Who was the intended audience of the plagues? The Egyptians? Moses? The Israelites? What do we make of a God who redeems a people by inflicting misery upon another? There are more questions about the plagues than there are plagues.

As I reread the plague cycle in the book of Exodus, I stumbled upon an aspect of them that I had never noticed before. There is a critical difference between the first three plagues – blood, frogs, and lice – and the other seven. The first three plagues afflicted all the inhabitants of the land equally – Egyptian, Israelite, rich, poor, near the Nile, in Goshen – everyone, everywhere. It wasn't just Pharaoh who awoke with frogs on his nose and frogs on his toes; it was everybody. And through these first three plagues, Pharaoh's resolve only stiffened; he would not let the Israelites go – not for three days, and certainly not for good.

It was only with the fourth plague – *arov*, usually translated as swarming insects – that God, through Moses, changed tactics. Listen to the language: "On that day, I will set apart the region of Goshen, where My people dwell, so that no swarms of insects shall be there... and I will make a distinction between My people and your people...." (Exodus 8:18–19) In other words, Moses announces, the Egyptians would be infested by the insects, but the Israelites would not. Which is exactly what happened. It was a display not only of God's mighty destructive power, but of one population being afflicted and another spared. The results were immediate. For the first time, for a short time, Pharaoh wavered: "Go and sacrifice to your God." (18:21) The Exodus itself was still a long time off. It would take more plagues – hail, darkness, the death of the firstborn. One group targeted, the other one spared. The point is made explicit in the plague of darkness: "People could not see one another, for three days no [Egyptian] could get up from where he was; but all the Israelites enjoyed light in their dwellings." (10:23) It is an intriguing thought, one I had never fully considered until this year. Had the plagues befallen everyone equally, we could not say *dayenu*.

That alone would *not* have been enough. Only by differentiating between communities, by targeting one community and not another would God deliver the full terror of the plagues. That was, if you will, the eleventh plague, the *coup de grace*, the one that made all the difference. Not hail, not darkness, not even the death of the firstborn, but the horrible realization that the destruction was not distributed equally among the inhabitants of the land. That is what broke Pharaoh's will.

Despite what Madonna may have tweeted out to the world, it seems to me that the coronavirus is not "the great equalizer." As with the plagues of the Passover story, our horror is amplified by knowing that whatever the ravages of the coronavirus may be, its ramifications – medically, socially, economically – are not felt equally by everyone. Of course, our community has been hit hard; I can no longer keep track of the number of synagogue members and family members who have either tested positive or are presumed positive. As evidenced by the long list of bereavements, our synagogue is not immune. The number of deaths, I believe, reflects a healthcare system stretched beyond capacity, hospitals forced to prioritize urgent care, and the elderly and ill lacking support systems that would enable the frail to withstand the virus despite their infirmities.

But I also know that terrible as the hour may be, my family and I are among the fortunate. Access to healthcare, access to food – these are privileges that many do not enjoy. To be able to socially distance, to work from home, to be able to work at all. I was telling someone about the all-consuming efforts made these past weeks to transform our synagogue into a virtual community, not to mention the pastoral demands this crisis imposes on clergy. This person reflected back that at the very least I was blessed to be in a position that is, for better or for worse, in demand. After all, to be busy and purposefully deployed is a blessing that many people sheltered in place do not enjoy.

The other day, I shared with a friend the good news and the bad news that I was ordering dinner in that evening. The good news was that I was ordering in – putting a restaurant and deliveryman to work. The bad news was that I was ordering in – putting a restaurant and deliveryman to work. I have the luxury of debating the relative merits of this choice and others, and if you are watching services this morning from your home, odds are that you do, too. But there is a world out there of people who do not. This virus is not hitting everyone equally. It is laying bare racial, ethnic, and economic inequities. It is bringing into stark relief so many societal fault lines that we would rather avoid – poverty, access to healthcare, food instability, and others. As I have shared many times from the pulpit, my family and I have the tradition of sitting at the Shabbat table every week and sharing our "roses and thorns," the best and worst parts of our week gone by. When it was my turn, my rose was that we were together, healthy, and under one roof. My thorn was that I knew that my blessings were not shared by so many members of humanity.

And this brings us back to the plagues. If the most frightful aspect of the plagues is the realization that they affected different communities differently, then perhaps the redemptive charge of this Passover is to work to close the gap between communities. Isn't that the whole point of this festival anyway? To remember that we were once strangers in a strange land and then leverage that realization toward addressing the condition of those standing at the periphery waiting to be redeemed. It is why decades ago we remembered and mobilized on behalf of Soviet and Syrian and Ethiopian Jewry. It is why as Jews we are uniquely sensitive – not just on Passover but year round – to the plight of immigrants, refugees, and anyone seeking liberation from oppression, be it ethnic, economic, gender, sexual, or any other kind. We recall the Exodus as if we ourselves left Egypt in order to raise in ourselves an abiding empathy for others: to feel empathy and to act on that empathy. This year, those of us like myself, perhaps like you, who are among the "haves," not the "have-nots," need to respond with deeds in keeping with our people's spiritual DNA. Give charitably; give blood, time, political resources; give of what you have. Give of yourself in a manner that addresses the acute needs of the hour and lays the foundation for a society that seeks to narrow, not widen, the systemic gaps between the diverse pockets of humanity created in God's image.

Finally, there is something that we all can do and must do, no matter who we are. As Klinenberg himself has written of late, it is unfortunate that in our efforts to flatten the spread of this deadly affliction, we have adopted the language of "social distancing." What we need, Klinenberg writes, is not "social distancing" but "physical distancing." If there is one thing the Chicago Heat Wave and all such crises have taught us, it is that the difference between life and death is not "social distancing," but "social solidarity." We may or may not have the means to contribute meaningfully to a charity; we may or may not feel comfortable putting ourselves in harm's way. But I do believe that all of us have the ability to pick up the phone and check in on each other and on the infirm and the elderly, to let people know that we are thinking of them, that we look forward to seeing them soon, please God, that they are not forgotten, and that if need be, we will help them identify how to get assistance.

That is my challenge to you: Don't just sit there. Yesterday we began to count the Omer –today is the second day – 49 days total between now and Shavuot, a stretch of time, the Talmud explains, that another terrible plague afflicted our people. Start this evening. Tack a piece of paper on your wall, write the names down – no less than one person per day. A phone call, an email – your choice – especially to people you may otherwise not reach out to. Why? Because odds are it is those folks that are not being checked in on by anyone else either. Social solidarity has nothing to do with liking people or being friends with them. Social solidarity is about creating a caring community and caring society, something that I hope we can all work toward. It may just make all the difference in the wilderness ahead.

April 11, 2020
17 Nisan 5780

"Dying Alone," Interview with Eric Klinenberg, University of Chicago Press, 2002
    https://www.press.uchicago.edu/Misc/Chicago/443213in.html

Sh'mini
On Leadership

It was precisely this week, in April of 1963, that Martin Luther King Jr. sat in a Birmingham, Alabama jail cell drafting what would become our nation's perhaps most treasured literary and moral document. Together with Ralph Abernathy and about fifty others, King had sought to leverage an Easter season boycott to integrate the downtown stores of Birmingham. King's non-violent protest march got only a few blocks before they were arrested and King put in solitary confinement. As you may recall, while King's letter addressed the scourge of racism, discrimination, and injustice, its ostensible audience was neither Alabama's Governor George Wallace, nor for that matter any of the obvious perpetrators of segregationist policy. The cause of King's ire was a letter printed in the Birmingham newspaper signed by eight local white clergymen – ministers, priests, bishops, and a rabbi – self-described racial moderates who critiqued King for his extreme, unwise, and untimely protests – outsider methods that could precipitate violence.

In the estimation of many, King's letter is comparable in stature to the Gettysburg Address and Zola's *J'accuse*; a *cri de coeur* against leaders who are hypocrites with respect to their own value systems. King takes his colleagues to task for their do-nothing leadership, having "almost reached the regrettable conclusion that the Negro's great stumbling block in his stride toward freedom is not the White Citizen's Counciler or the Ku Klux Klanner but the white moderate, who is more devoted to 'order' than to justice . . ." King railed against those who "remain[ed] silent behind the anesthetizing security of stained-glass windows," predicting that ". . . we will have to repent in this generation not merely for the hateful words and actions of the bad people but for the appalling silence of the good people." It was not only that, as Heschel would later say, "indifference to evil is worse than evil itself." Rather, it was that these leaders failed to represent the very traditions, texts, values, and ideals that they preached and taught and that their clerical calling demanded they embody. Did they not know their scripture, their prophetic calling, the shared Judeo-Christian insistence to create a just society? I can think of no better way to mark the anniversary of King's "Letter from a Birmingham Jail" than to spend some time this weekend rereading it, reading what is perhaps the greatest smackdown against hypocrisy in leadership: leaders who talk the talk but fail to walk the walk.

Aside from the anniversary of King's letter, according to the Jewish calendar we are in the midst of the *sefirah*, which means "counting," specifically the days between the festivals of Passover and Shavuot. If you are unfamiliar with the observance, also known as "the counting of the Omer," it involves counting each day between our liberation from Egypt and the receiving of the law forty-nine days later at Mount Sinai. This year, as you may know, I am urging each of you to count off each day with at least one phone call to a person who would benefit from a check-in – a modest gesture of social solidarity during this time of physical distancing. By a certain telling, it is a joyous time of year as our people, both ancient and modern, eagerly anticipate the gift of God's Torah.

What you may not know (and what explains my misshapen facial scruff), is that according to tradition, this period of time is also understood by many as a time for sober reflection. The Talmud (Yevamot 62b), records that it was precisely during these weeks that twelve thousand pairs of Rabbi Akiva's students died – felled by a plague. In many Jewish communities, despite the anticipated arrival at Mount Sinai, this is a somber time of year. Weddings are not performed and certain aspects of mourning, like not shaving, are observed.

For me, the most important aspect of the mournful character of the *sefirah* has always been the question "why?" Why were Rabbi Akiva's students punished as they were? What misstep, what wrong, what crime did they commit to justify such a punishment? The Talmud states only *lo nahagu kavod zeh bazeh*, they didn't treat each other with *kavod*, that is, with respect. Over time, subsequent commentators have read into the Talmud's terse language a more fatal leadership flaw of Rabbi Akiva's students. Rabbi Akiva, as you may know, was the greatest representative of Torah in his day, and his students, more than anyone else, were expected to be living exemplars of Torah. They were the teachers, the guardians of tradition, responsible for modeling behavior for others to emulate. But they didn't treat each other with respect. The gravity of their failing was compounded because their behavior was not only a personal failing but also a leadership failure to represent the very ideals that they were called on to embody. All the time, but especially during this time prior to celebrating the receiving of the law, a person is expected to narrow, not widen, the gap between what one says and what one does. For Rabbi Akiva's students it was the dissonance, the disconnect, between what they said and what they did – between the talk they talked and the walk they walked – that brought on their catastrophic punishment.

There are, to be sure, many measures of leadership. The courage and charisma needed to stand before a Pharaoh. The empathy required to understand the needs of those one leads. The emotional intelligence necessary to respond instinctually to the demands of the moment whether expected or unforeseen. But from Moses to Machiavelli to Martin Luther King Jr., perhaps the most important and most enduring measurement of a leader is the degree to which a leader not just talks the talk but also walks the walk. "We are," wrote Aristotle, "what we repeatedly do." It is by way of our deeds, not our words, that we rise and fall, a thought that once led Emerson to reflect, "What you *are* shouts so loudly in my ears, I cannot hear what you *say*." Of the three types of people whom the Talmud relates that God hates, the first is *"eḥad b'peh v'eḥad b'lev,"* a person who says one thing and does another, in other words, a person who does not practice what they preach.

This criterion, I believe, helps us understand the enigmatic and seemingly unjustified death of Aaron's two sons Nadav and Avihu, which we read about in this morning's Torah portion. None of the reasons offered by the rabbis – arrogance, disrespect of Moses and Aaron, a licentious lifestyle, or anything else – fully explains their sudden and tragic demise. Their fatal misstep, if you will, was not any one thing they did; rather, it was that they had forgotten that their position called on them to represent not just themselves, but also something much bigger – God. This is the only way to understand God's justification for their deaths: *Bikrovai akadesh*, Through those near to me, I will be made holy. (Leviticus 10:3) In other words, while everyone should aspire toward consistency between word and action, it is a responsibility that falls especially on those who represent something more than their own personhood. Indeed, the close reader will hear echoes of our parashah soon enough when we read of Moses being barred from entering the promised land for the misstep of striking rather than speaking to the rock. Unto itself, Moses's punishment is totally disproportionate to his misdeed. Yet, in light of Moses's stature as a leader, his wrong behavior was enough to preclude his entering the promised land. It seems there is a relationship between a leader's stature and the expectations we have for their behavior.

"A good leader," I recently read, "tries to embody the best qualities of his or her organization. A good leader sets the example for others to follow. A good leader always puts the welfare of others before himself or herself." By extension, a leader who fails to show these qualities represents a failing not just of an individual, but of the ideals that leader professes to embody. The consistency between what one says and does, the walk and the talk – that one does not expect of others what one does not expect of oneself – this is the measure by which leaders make or miss the mark. Examples from history abound – in both directions. Dr. King and the clergymen, Aaron's sons, Moses and the rock. General Eisenhower, who famously drafted a letter of resignation prior to the Normandy invasion, stating, that in the event of failure, ". . . any blame or fault attached to the attempt . . . is mine alone." The stakes need not be life or death. The leadership of Derek Jeter was not based merely on his athleticism and talent; it was his ability to work as hard if not harder than anyone else and thus inspire others to follow, that made him "the captain."

At all times, but especially in times of crisis, the behavior of leaders sets the culture of the people and the institutions they lead. And ours is such a time. A time for every individual and every institution that contributes toward setting culture to speak and act in a manner befitting the demands of the hour. Given our goal to flatten the curve of this plague of our generation, all of us, individually and institutionally, must comport ourselves accordingly and model the behavior we would ask of others. Given the social and economic stress being inflicted on our social fabric, it is incumbent upon us all to adopt a spirit of sacrifice commensurate with the magnitude of our present crisis. It is not enough simply to reflect on the sort of public conversation we wish to see. In this hour we must act in accord with our ideals, creating consistency between our words and actions and demanding the same consistency from all those in leadership positions.

Some of you may be listening today and thinking, "I agree with you, rabbi, but I am not a leader. I don't run an institution; I am not a bearer of culture. Your sermon does not apply to me." I ask you to think again. Because no matter the scale, no matter the context in which you live – in your family, your workplace, your home – you are an exemplar. The degree to which you demonstrate patience, kindness, compassion, creativity, a collaborative spirit, a spirit of sacrifice, a spirit of transparent communication is an unspoken signal to those around you. At all times, but especially in times like this, it is the smallest gestures that speak volumes. Each one of us has both the opportunity and the obligation to be our best selves, for ourselves and for others to follow.

This past week, I had occasion to revisit a 2014 commencement address delivered to the graduates of the University of Texas by Admiral William McRaven, the retired United States four-star Navy admiral. The admiral shared the lessons he learned from SEAL training that made him the leader he would grow to become. His speech that day went on to become a book that I recommend in full. Today I share with you his first lesson. McRaven states:

> "Every morning in basic SEAL training, my instructors... would show up in my barracks... and the first thing they would inspect was your bed. If you did it right, the corners would be square, the covers pulled tight, the pillow centered just under the headboard and the extra blanket folded neatly at the foot of the rack....
>
> "It was a simple task – mundane at best. But every morning we were required to make our bed to perfection. It seemed a little ridiculous at the time, particularly in light of the fact that we were aspiring to be real warriors, tough battle-hardened SEALs, but the wisdom of this simple act has been proven to me many times over.
>
> "If you make your bed every morning you will have accomplished the first task of the day. It will give you a small sense of pride, and it will encourage you to do another task and another and another. By the end of the day, that one task completed will have turned into many tasks completed. Making your bed will also reinforce the fact that little things in life matter. If you can't do the little things right, you will never do the big things right.
>
> "And, if by chance you have a miserable day, you will come home to a bed that is made – that you made – and a made bed gives you encouragement that tomorrow will be better.
>
> "If you want to change the world, start off by making your bed."

Friends, some people lead institutions, some people lead countries, and some people are just trying their level best to make their beds. But we can all lead. We can all live by a consistency of deed and action – in the big things and the little things – improving our lot, the lot of those around us, and the lot of the world in which we live. It is not enough, in the journey in which we find ourselves, merely to talk the talk. We need to walk the walk, step by step, each one of us an embodiment of the ideals we profess to hold dear, slowly, courageously and collectively mending this world in such urgent need of repair.

April 18, 2020
24 Nisan 5780

McRaven, William, Commencement Address, University of Texas 2014
   https://news.utexas.edu/2014/05/16/mcraven-urges-graduates-to-find-courage-to-change-the-world/

Tazri·a/M'tzora

The Life and Legacy of Waldemar M.W. Haffkine

I have to imagine that when Waldemar Haffkine (1860-1930) heard this morning's Torah reading, *Tazri·a/M'tzora*, it brought a smile to his face. After all, to the degree that there is a biblical precedent to WebMD, this week's parashah is it: ancient Israel's medical textbook on how to diagnose and address the outbreak of a plague. In the time of the Torah, the *kohen*, the priest, was both the religious and the medical authority of the community, the urgent care professional consulted when a person was afflicted with a debilitating condition. Our Torah reading describes how the *kohen* would visit the afflicted, examine them, diagnose their condition, and, based on what he saw, prescribe a course of action. But the *kohen* was more than a first responder; he was also a public health official. The afflicted individual was isolated and put into quarantine as the broader community was informed of the outbreak. Had the plague spread throughout the household? Beyond that single home? Depending on the answer, extra measures were mandated for anyone who came into contact with the afflicted, and depending how bad things were, that person's house could even be torn down. Finally, in his quasi-governmental role, the priest would signal the path by which an individual, once healed, could be reintegrated into society and society itself returned to normalcy. For young Waldemar Haffkine, a man who would spend his life in the enterprise of eradicating deadly plagues, *Tazri·a/M'tzora* must have been the scriptural and spiritual foundation for the ventures and adventures that would become his life work.

This morning I want to offer a different kind of sermon. I want to tell you about Waldemar Haffkine, a man whom I would guess most of you know nothing about, someone about whom I knew nothing until I began to do a little digging into one of the most underappreciated, inspiring, and tragic figures in the history of epidemiology. I dedicate this sermon in honor of the medical professionals serving on the front lines of our present-day public health crisis.

Our story begins, as do so many Jewish stories, in czarist Russia, Odessa to be precise, where Waldemar Mordecai Wolff Haffkine was born in the year 1860 – the same year, interestingly, as Theodore Herzl. Waldemar's mother died when he was eight, and his father, a struggling merchant, enrolled young Waldemar in a local school at the age of ten. At the age of nineteen, he entered Odessa's Faculty of Natural Science to study zoology under Élie Metchnikoff, a future Nobel prize winner in the field of immunology.

If you know your Jewish history, then you know that 1880s Russia was not an easy time or place for Jews. The antisemitic pogroms that broke out following the assassination of Czar Alexander II in St. Petersburg took a terrible toll on our people, with many Jews emigrating westward and a far smaller number following their hearts eastward in what would be the first wave of immigration, the first Aliyah, to Palestine.

Haffkine himself dreamt of social revolution, and although he was not personally involved in the assassination plot, he was a card-carrying member of the terrorist revolutionary group *Narodnay Volya* (The Will of the People) that was. Young Haffkine was not a religious man, though he did have a strong sense of Jewish peoplehood and was a member of the Jewish League for Self Defense. Not surprisingly, given his activism, Haffkine was expelled from university twice and arrested three times by the Russian authorities, released only on account of the intervention of his mentor, Professor Metchnikoff.

Principled as he was, Haffkine refused to convert to Christianity, a choice that would have paved the way toward his attaining a coveted professorship. He came to understand that he would have to leave Russia in order to advance his research career. At the time, Paris-based

Louis Pasteur was opening up an entire branch of science to combat the devastating cholera outbreaks that were ravaging Asia and Europe. In 1888, Haffkine arranged passage from Russia to Switzerland and eventually, by 1890, he arrived in Paris where his old mentor Metchnikoff was working in the newly opened Pasteur Institute.

It is here where our story really begins. But before we step forward, we need to take a small step back to provide context for those of you, like myself, who have no medical training. In the face of an outbreak of infectious disease, there are – broadly speaking – two baskets of response. The responses in the first basket aim to control the epidemic, which, aside from preventive public health measures like sanitation and physical distancing, as prescribed by our parashah and our governor, is the world of inoculations. Think Edward Jenner and the smallpox vaccine, Jonas Salk and the polio vaccine, and the common flu shot. The second basket of responses aims to control the disease itself – the steps one takes to arrest and ease the symptoms of the afflicted with the goal of reducing the mortality rate. Think the discovery of penicillin by the great Scotsman Alexander Fleming; streptomycin by the American Jew Selman Waksman, which stemmed the devastating toll of tuberculosis; or our present-day efforts aimed to treat COVID-19. When I was a kid, my mother would kick me and my brothers out of the house on a Sunday so she could have some peace and quiet, and we would all go hang out in my dad's doctor's office. I remember watching him placing a patient's bacteria sample onto a culture plate with tiny discs of antibiotics; he would then incubate the slide and then measure the circular area around the antibiotic in order to determine which one could combat the bacterial infection, something called the zone of inhibition, the technical name for the measure by which bacteria colonies grow, or, in retrospect, by which children of doctors are inhibited from growing into doctors themselves.

Haffkine's interest was in the first category: he was a prophet of prophylactic inoculations. Through a series of networking moves worthy of Joseph in Pharaoh's court, he figured out a way to get himself – a Jew from Odessa – sent in 1893 by the British government to India, which was suffering from a fifth devastating outbreak of cholera, which had killed millions. Haffkine's efforts to develop a vaccine were opposed by local officials who were understandably suspect of his motives, and he survived an assassination attempt by Islamic extremists. No medical research could be possible without human trials, so Haffkine actually inoculated himself with live mitigated cholera bacteria, and though he suffered fever and discomfort, to make a long story short, he was eventually able to gain the trust of his colleagues and local Indian leadership. By 1895, tens of thousands of people had been inoculated, saving countless lives. His success was overwhelming, but Haffkine was exhausted and had contracted malaria along the way. He returned home to Europe, where he was showered with praise for his self-sacrifice, scientific zeal, and courage of conviction, with Haffkine himself attributing all of his success to Louis Pasteur.

Here is where things get really interesting... and tragic. In 1896, Haffkine returned to India, this time not on account of cholera but for the scourge of plague that had broken out in India by way of a rat-infested ship from Hong Kong. Working fourteen-hour days, Haffkine once again set up a laboratory in order to create a vaccine, which, once it proved successful in animals, he then used on himself, as was his custom. Though far from perfect, his vaccine worked, diminishing the death rate from the plague by as much as 80 or 90 percent. Haffkine's plague prophylactic was improved upon and administered throughout India, his work saving millions of lives. Throughout it all, in all these years, Haffkine's devotion to his people never wavered. In the early 1890s he founded a society for the revival of the Hebrew Language. He supported the efforts to open a plague hospital for Jews of all denominations in Bombay. Perhaps most interestingly, he worked behind the scenes to urge the Turkish Sultan to settle Jews in Palestine, corresponding with Baron Edmond James de Rothschild on the goal of establishing a Jewish homeland.

So where is the tragedy? It came in 1902. Five batches of Haffkine's plague vaccine produced in his Bombay lab in September arrived in the village of Mulkowal in the Punjab in November, and nineteen patients died after receiving the vaccine from one contaminated flask, number 53n. Haffkine was suspended from his post and pay and then endured a four-year investigation, which held him culpable. Eventually, the truth emerged that it would have been physically impossible for the contamination to have occurred in Haffkine's lab months before the injections took place. Rather, the contamination had actually happened when an assistant at the Mulkowal lab dropped his forceps on the ground and then used the non-sterile instrument. But that truth came out only years later. As explained by Marina Sorikina, Haffkine's "origin and independent scientific, civil and religious views did not find acceptance within the British colonial bureaucracy." ("Between Faith and Reason: Waldemar Haffkine (1860-1930) in India," p. 175) Haffkine, together with some of his defenders, mounted a vigorous defense, eventually leading to the overturning of the decision and his exoneration and reinstatement in 1907. Unofficially, the inquiry commission was referred to as the "Little Dreyfus Affair," a reference to the Jewish French military officer falsely accused of treason a few years earlier. Haffkine returned to India in 1908, but by then, as in the Dreyfus case, the damage had been done. The stigma of the Mulkowal disaster remained; the terms of Haffkine's employment were restricted; and his research activities were curtailed. Only one of the fifteen papers he wrote over his lifetime was published during these years. Upon reaching the minimum retirement age of 55 in 1915, he left the Indian civil service entirely.

From 1915 until his death in 1930, Haffkine lived a quiet life, largely ignored by the scientific community. He turned his attention to Jewish causes; having been deprived throughout his career of intimacy with his kinsmen, he wanted to return to his faith. He traveled around Europe and America seeking to establish schools of Jewish learning in Palestine and the diaspora that could bridge the gap between faith and reason. Having never returned to his hometown in forty years, he paid a final visit to Odessa. He wrote a fascinating article on Jewish identity and the nature of Jewish peoplehood that was later canonized in the commentary of the famous Hertz Pentateuch. When Haffkine died in Switzerland in 1930, he left his entire estate of 1.5 million francs (about half a million dollars) toward fostering religious, scientific, and vocational education in Eastern European yeshivas, stipulating that their curricula be expanded "so that [their students] not be reduced to misery and begging," a tragic legacy given what we know was the ultimate fate of his beneficiaries just a few years later.

The life of Waldemar Mordechai Wolff Haffkine – a journey from revolutionary to life-saving epidemiologist to maligned Jew to scholar-philanthropist. It took years for Haffkine's legacy to be restored. Eventually he would be honored by the Bombay plague research laboratory renamed in his honor; a few stamps, Israeli and Indian, issued with his picture; a memorial grove in Jerusalem planted in his memory; a laboratory flask bearing his name; and yes, millions and millions of people who would not have been born had it not been for him.

This, I suppose, is the enduring legacy and altogether relevant message of Haffkine for us today. In this moment, when we stand face-to-face with a pandemic the likes of which we have never contended with before, we would do well to pause, to consider, and to reflect with gratitude for those doctors, nurses, healthcare professionals, researchers, and others whose dedicated commitment to the preservation of life speaks to our highest ideals – not just as Jews but as human beings. As one attendee reflected at Haffkine's funeral: "Great was his scientific work in that he literally saved millions of lives, but equally great was the personal character of the man, and most particularly, his modesty and humility. He never asked for help from any man but he was always ready to help others and befriend the needy." That is an epitaph to which anyone devoted to the advancement of medicine should aspire. For that matter, it is a description that any human being would be lucky to earn. As Longfellow wrote, the lives of great men and women remind us that we too can make our lives sublime. Waldemar Haffkine was such a man. May his memory inspire us to aspire to the same for ourselves.

April 25, 2020
1 Iyyar 5780

Sources Consulted and for Further Reading

Haffkine, Waldemar M. "A Plea for Orthodoxy," *The Menorah Journal*, 2:2 (April 1916)
>https://www.google.com/books/edition/_/iKhCr05rxIYC?hl=en&gbpv=1&pg=PA67&dq=plea+for+orthodoxy+menorah+journal+1916

Jhala, H.I. "W.M.W. Haffkine, Bacteriologist – A Great Savior of Mankind" in *Indian Journal of History of Science 2:105–20* (November 1967)
>http://insa.nic.in/writeraddata/UpLoadedFiles/IJHS/Vol02_2_2HIJhala.pdf

Lutzker, E. "The Curious Case of Waldemar Haffkine," *Commentary*, 69:6 (June 1980)
>https://www.commentarymagazine.com/articles/edythe-lutzker/the-curious-history-of-waldemar-haffkine/z

Sorokina, M. "Between Faith and Reason: Waldemar Haffkine (1860-1930) in India"
>https://www.researchgate.net/publication/267247263_Between_Faith_and_Reason_Waldemar_Haffkine_1860-1930_in_India_Western_Jews_in_India_From_the_Fifteenth_Century_to_the_Present_Ed_By_Wenneth_X_Robbins_Marvin_Tokayer_Delhi_Manohar_2013_P_161-178

Waksman, S. *The Brilliant and Tragic Life of W.M.W. Haffkine, Bacteriologist* (New Brunswick, NJ: Rutgers University Press, 1964)

Aḥarei Mot/K'doshim
Like I Told You, It's an Honor

In the storied history of journalism, the column Jimmy Breslin published in *The New York Herald Tribune* on November 26, 1963, stands as one of the most memorable newspaper articles of all time. The piece is entitled "It's an Honor," and if you know your history, then you know it was published following the assassination and funeral of President John F. Kennedy.

Breslin's article, studied to this day in schools of journalism, attained acclaim not because it described our nation's grief, delved into the implications of a head of state being killed, or for that matter, assessed President Kennedy's legacy. Breslin's article was remarkable because it was written about a gravedigger at Arlington National Cemetery, Clifton Pollard, the man who prepared President Kennedy's grave. Breslin, who passed away in 2017 at the age of 88, would later recall: "I [went] to the White House and there [were] three thousand reporters.... I can't work with that. I decide[d] I am going to get the guy who is going to dig the grave." So, as every other journalist covered a nation in mourning, Breslin found his own angle, writing about Kennedy's funeral from the gravedigger's perspective: the call he received to come to work that morning as he was eating his bacon and eggs; the reverse hoe he used to dig the grave; and the quality of the soil itself. The $3.01 per hour wage Pollard earned as "one of the last to serve John Fitzgerald Kennedy." Above all, the sense of honor Pollard felt in quietly shouldering his duty. Breslin's article concluded with Pollard's own words: ". . . like I told you, it's an honor." Breslin made the small big, reminding his readers of the human story outside the spotlight, a story that would otherwise have been missed.

This morning, I would like to share with you the human story of the last two months. Not an analysis of our global pandemic, not policy prescriptions, and certainly not politics. I want to speak personally, pastorally, as a rabbi, as your rabbi, on behalf of all the PAS clergy, who have been caring for our community, grieving with our community, and supporting our community during this time of unprecedented loss. The numbers, as you have seen in our bereavement emails, are staggering – an exponential increase in deaths in our community compared to this time last year. Members of our community, the loved ones of members, and the loved ones of our synagogue staff family. Many of those lost have been afflicted by COVID-19. Many are what I call, for lack of a precise term, "COVID-adjacent" deaths, meaning the passing of infirm or elderly individuals due to lack of medical or social attention, or because the hospital system is so overwhelmed that it has been forced to prioritize urgent care in unprecedented ways. The precipitous decline and death of individuals who in normal circumstances might have lived longer.

Our parashah this week is *Aharei Mot/K'doshim*, meaning "After Death/Holiness." In the spirit of Jimmy Breslin, this morning I want to share not the numbers, but the stories of our communal loss. *Aharei Mot/K'doshim*, after death, holiness: stories of after death, death itself, and perhaps most painfully, and where we shall begin, *lifnei mot*, before death.

Such things should not be ranked, but I have found the cruelest aspect of our communal losses to be the experiences *lifnei mot*, before or preceding death. My thoughts turn to the father of one congregant who had not been feeling himself and who went to the hospital accompanied by his wife of fifty years. She sat in the waiting room as tests were conducted. A medical professional came, greeted her, and handed over her husband's cell phone and personal effects, instructing her to go home: he had tested positive. All she wanted was to stay at his side, to be with him as she had for the last fifty years, but it was not to be. I think of another congregational family having to make end-of-life decisions for the family patriarch dying in a hospital room. In my experience as a rabbi, there is nothing more heartbreaking than a family conversation on whether to withhold care for a loved one, except having to make those decisions from a distance. I have never, until this month, had to recite the death-bed prayer to a person over the phone, and I hope I will never have to do so ever again. I think of one individual, a Holocaust survivor who had survived Buchenwald and Bergen-Belsen, who had rebuilt his life in America – blessed with four children, ten grandchildren and four great-grandchildren – who died last week without his family at his side. I think of two other congregants who died alone. In both cases, without next of kin, we arranged their burials with their lawyers and representatives. Death is cruel enough as it is, but nobody – nobody – should ever die alone. It is not just the number of deaths, it is the nature of each person's passing that has taken a staggering toll on our congregational families and on all of us.

And if this is what precedes death, then the realities of death itself are equally shattering. Funerals, as any clergyperson knows, are the most intimate and moving times to be with families: grieving together, weaving the narrative of a loved one's life, and providing the family with the social support of the community. But for these last months, funeral services have been transformed. There are no public gatherings and no funeral services; everything happens at graveside. Plaza, Riverside – the funeral homes we work with – are doing the best they can given the sheer volume and backlog. Families are assigned a time slot – 2:00 pm on a Tuesday; 11:00 am on a Wednesday – you take what you are given. Every cemetery has its own rules. Some limit burials to just family, some to no more than five, some allow no family at all. Sometimes the rules change; you don't actually know until you get there. In order to protect the gravediggers, the mourners are required to remain in the car as the casket is lowered. Only then is the family given permission to go to the graveside. Brothers and sisters, spouses – standing at a distance with masks and gloves. There are no handshakes or hugs. Inevitably, one person is holding an iPhone so another can watch from a distance: a child or a sibling not present, who couldn't get on a plane or couldn't take the health risk. There is a Psalm, a word of Torah, and an opportunity for anyone to share a memory. There is no pomp or pageantry, no elegantly crafted eulogy, no playing the deceased's favorite song. Everything is from the heart, with raw, painful, free-flowing tears. In all its unfair inhumanity, there is something deeply authentic about it all. You cannot shovel earth, because that would require passing a shovel, so you grab a handful of earth – or three or ten – and you throw it in your loved one's final resting place. You recite kaddish and the memorial prayer, and then . . . you get back in the car. The service ends as abruptly as it began.

Post-burial Jewish rituals – shiva, shloshim, and otherwise – as the rabbis themselves understood, are meant both to honor the dead and comfort the bereaved. But the rabbis never imagined a moment like ours when public assembly is forbidden. Children are not reconvening in their parent's home for a meal. The community is forbidden from gathering; there is no minyan to recite kaddish. Many go home from the cemetery to an empty house. The enormity of a loved one's death takes time to take hold; shiva is one of the many mechanisms that help people absorb and accept loss. But if you go home alone, as several have reflected to me, the shock and disbelief linger razor-sharp. Without context or community to process, it doesn't actually feel real.

Under the circumstances, the synagogue has tried to do our best with online shiva. A time is set, a Zoom link created, an email sent, and an hour spent "together" online. With a combination of psalms read, memories shared, condolence notes written in the chat bar, and kaddish, it is part funeral and part memorial service. In all its stilted awkwardness, in all its deficiencies, it is not without merit. Loved ones gather from the four corners of the world, from across the span of a person's life, from childhood to college and through adulthood. Individuals who would otherwise never make it to shiva can make it to an online shiva. People share memories and, more importantly, people listen and can see other's faces in a way you just can't in a crowded room. Loved ones are honored and mourners are comforted. It is not the same – it is not nearly the same – and it is heartbreaking to think of the mourner staring at the blank screen when the Zoom session ends, but it is better than nothing. In fact, I wouldn't be at all surprised if in years to come, when life and death, please God, return to normal, mourners will announce hybrid shiva times, some in person and some on Zoom. COVID or no COVID, I would bet that Zoom shivas are here to stay, and I am not sure that is such a terrible thing.

For all the heartache and all the continued constraints, these past months have not been without moments of profound humanity. A man told me of the kindness of a hospice nurse who suited up in PPE just to place her phone next to his father's ear, as he and his daughters expressed their love for their father and grandfather, just minutes before his soul entered God's eternal embrace. I think of the graveside funeral of a man who had narrowly escaped the clutches of Nazi Germany, whose son found comfort in the knowledge that his father was granted proper burial, a *mitzvah* denied to the Six Million. I think of another graveside funeral one windy day, when the scribbled notes being read by a grandchild blew from his hands directly into his grandmother's grave. The moment could not have been scripted, and it granted the family so much comfort that every subsequent speaker placed their notes into the grave after speaking. I think of another funeral where health and geography prevented family from being present so photographs of everyone were lovingly placed in the grave. I think of the uplift one woman experienced upon entering a Zoom shiva as she realized the number of lives her father had touched. I think of one congregant, who, arriving at home after burying his brother, looked out his front window to see ten physically distanced members of our community standing outside to daven with him so he could recite kaddish. I am reminded of the old story attributed to the Maggid of Dubno about the king who had a diamond with a scratch on it, that no one could repair until a rabbi came and incorporated the scratch as the stem of a rose that he engraved on the diamond. We are a long way from being able to create beauty from the hurt and damage we are all suffering. But at the very least, I would like to think that even now all those scratches and cracks can let in the light of humanity and God. Even now there is holiness, *kedushah*, before death, in death, and after death.

As for me, these months have been filled with the most trying, exhausting, and rewarding stretch of my pastoral career. I am heartbroken that the pace has not permitted us to check in on the bereaved with greater frequency. We need bereavement groups led by social workers; we need volunteers to make check-in phone calls. Clergy need to reflect on how we can care better for our synagogue members even as we are off to respond to the next passing. We are far from perfect, and I will be the first to name our shortcomings. I would only ask for your patience and forgiveness as we try to do our best in this dark hour.

And in all of it, to be sure, I am reminded why I became a rabbi: to be brought into the confidence of people's lives with their humanity at its most raw; to be extended the opportunity to let the wisdom of our tradition ease a person's sorrow; to be present to remind people that even when they are most isolated, they are not alone. Excepting the health care professionals on the front line who are literally saving lives, I am hard pressed to think of a more worthwhile vocation. The clergy team, your clergy team, as always, stands ready to serve. Like I told you, it's an honor.

May 2, 2020
8 Iyyar 5780

Breslin, Jimmy. "Digging JFK Grave Was His Honor," *New York Herald Tribune*, November 1963.
    http://www.arlingtoncemetery.net/digging-grave-an-honor.htm

Emor
Dreams Deferred

Of late, I have found myself returning again and again to the opening line of a poem found in Langston Hughes's "Harlem," a poem made famous by Lorraine Hansberry's 1959 play, *A Raisin in the Sun*:

What happens to a dream deferred?

>Does it dry up
>Like a raisin in the sun?
>Or fester like a sore—
>And then run?
>Does it stink like rotten meat?
>Or crust and sugar over—
>Like a syrupy sweet?
>
>Maybe it just sags
>Like a heavy load.
>
>*Or does it explode?*

This short poem is one of about ninety riffing on Hughes's beloved Harlem and what Harlem represented in his mind and the minds of so many African Americans of his day who were yearning for individual achievement and America's supposed promise of equality. The poem, together with the montage of poems surrounding it, asks what happens to a person who discovers that their long-sought dreams are beyond reach. What happens to a dream deferred? Does it just shrivel up and go away? Does it linger and fester? Or does it – as Hughes suggests in his allusion to the Harlem riots – explode? The poem, as you may recall from your high school English class, continues to resonate throughout American culture. What happens when what we have anticipated, what we believe ourselves due and have worked so hard to achieve – through no fault of our own – proves unobtainable? From the speeches of Martin Luther King Jr. to Broadway to DREAM act legislation, it would not be an understatement to say that Hughes's brief be-bop modernist lyric is one of the most influential poems of twentieth-century America, if not the entire canon of American literature.

This morning, I find myself concerned not so much with my own high school experience, but the lives of an inestimable number of high school students, college students, early childhood, elementary, and junior high students: the present-day montage of dreams deferred due to COVID-19. It is, after all, the month of May, a time meant to be filled with proms and prom dresses, graduations and caps and gowns, moving-up ceremonies, end-of-year athletic playoffs, internships, and packing lists for summer camp. Everyone has been affected. Semesters abroad have been cancelled, job offers have been rescinded, and long-planned reunions put on hold. I think of the eleventh-grader who was looking forward to being scouted by college teams. I think of the ACT and SAT exams being rescheduled and the cascade of resulting implications. I think of the millions of regretful decisions that are every teenager's right to make but are being presently denied them. The other day my daughter stoically shared with me that her final day to be together with her high school class had come and gone without her realizing it at the time. I was supposed to officiate at a wedding this coming week and one the following week and another the week after that – so many simchas being rescheduled. Sometimes life gives us second chances; yesterday, after all, was Pesach Sheni, a biblical redo for those who missed making the Pesach sacrifice the first time around. But you and I both know that not everything can be redone. Many dreams have been deferred, and an equal if not greater number have been derailed and denied, never to be rescheduled.

The sense of loss, of course, is not just about our children and grandchildren. It is about all of us: the loss of stability, predictability, and reliability. The very scaffolding of our existence has come undone. The rhythm of our days is upended, from the most mundane acts – the risk vs. reward of stepping into a subway – to the most weighty decisions – to change jobs, leave an unhappy marriage, or bring another child into this world. People on the verge of retirement are now needing to work longer, for themselves and for their children and grandchildren. If you stop, really stop, to consider the number of dreams deferred by our dark hour, the thought can suffocate. And it is a thought made even heavier by the knowledge that the road ahead is so uncertain. We just don't know if and how campus life will resume in the fall; we don't know what vaccines are on the horizon. I recently read about a category of loss called "anticipatory grief," the feeling we get when the future is so uncertain. None of us know when the light will appear at the end of the tunnel. Like passengers on ships lined up off-shore waiting to find safe harbor, our heartache is not just about what has been lost, but about being stalled in place as the calendar moves inexorably forward into an unclear future.

So what shall we say in response to dreams deferred? We have no solutions; we have no crystal ball. But people are in pain; we need a response. What shall we say to our children and grandchildren? What shall we say to each other? What shall we say to ourselves?

It is not an easy question to answer, so let me begin by suggesting what not to say, how not to respond when your kid learns that camp is cancelled, when your friend shares that her wedding is postponed, or your nephew graduates college without a job. First, avoid drawing from what I call the "at least you are not dead" basket:

"So your program was cancelled – read the news, people are fighting for their lives!"

"Sorry you have to take the SAT next fall – but at least you have a roof over your head."

There are certain moments in life when the first words out of your mouth really matter: When someone gets engaged, you say, *"Mazel tov!"* When a new parent tells you the name of their baby, you say, "I love it." When my wife asks me if I like a dress, "I do!" Most often, there will be time to redirect and recalibrate, but you get only one chance for a first response. And when someone is suffering, do not respond by spotlighting weightier losses. It may come from a good place, it may even be an intellectually defensible position, but an indelicate "at least you are not dead" response makes a person feel that you don't find their pain to be real. I thought long and hard about whether to give a sermon about the loss of high school graduation and other such deferred dreams when people are on ventilators. I decided I had to, because not to would be an omission which in itself would invalidate the world of pain that so many are experiencing right now. Rule number one of first response to a person's loss: Don't tell them that in the big scheme of things they are lucky.

The "at least you are not dead" basket of responses takes on many forms, some more subtle than others. There is the "imagine what it was like" variation: Imagine what it was like to be born in the Depression, to be part of the Greatest Generation, or, for Jews, to have lived through any number of pogroms or persecutions. Again, it may be true that someone else in another time and place has also suffered, but when I am in pain, is that really going to help me? It is a bit like when I was kid and I would complain to my dad (a physician, by the way) that my ear hurt, and he would pinch my arm and ask, "Now what hurts?" It didn't make me feel better when I was a kid and it didn't make my kids feel any better when I did it to them. You can't tell a kid that it was never about receiving a diploma on graduation day, but about the accomplishment leading up to that day, because in that kid's mind, at that moment, it is all about the diploma. You can hold these thoughts in your head, just don't share them – not yet and possibly not ever.

Another category of response to be avoided is the "silver lining" basket. Camp is cancelled – what a great time to take up an instrument or start studying for your ACT! Today is that rainy day, that block of downtime you've been waiting for: to read that book, to take up that pet project, to learn chess, to lose five pounds, or to finally learn how to mix a margarita. Again, it may be true, and it may even be good advice. Just don't say it to a person as they stare eye-to-eye at a dream deferred. We are all familiar with the "What doesn't kill you makes you stronger" response: telling someone how the best things in life happen in response to setback. Perhaps, but generally speaking, when a door slams in a person's face, they are not ready to hear about the ten that just opened. Similarly, to suggest that this crisis will prompt us to reexamine our priorities, teaching us what is really important – the fragility of life, to treat the environment with greater care – is also fraught with problems. I am reminded of the Talmudic exchange between Rabbi Yohanan and Rabbi Hiyya, who was lying ill. Rabbi Yohanan asked Rabbi Hiyya if his suffering was dear to him, to which Rabbi Hiyya replied, "I welcome neither my suffering nor its reward." (Babylonian Talmud Berakhot 5b) Not all lemons produce lemonade, and like Rabbi Hiyya, I personally would forgo any silver linings if doing so could avoid our present world of hurt. I have no idea if the pandemic will make us stronger as a society or if it will break us, if it will pass soon or prove to be our enduring new normal. All I do know is that we do ourselves and our loved ones a terrible disservice by sugarcoating pain with pithy bromides.

So what can we say? What can we say that does not risk pablum or platitude, that is not tone-deaf or insensitive? Rather than tell you what I think, I will tell you what one of my kids thinks, words spoken to me when I asked what a parent should say if summer camp is cancelled. My kid said:

> "Dad, what I need to hear, what every kid needs to hear, is an acknowledgement of the pain of the situation. Let me know that you know how much this sucks. Don't tell me to move on. Don't tell me that other people are suffering more. I have looked forward to summer all year for eight years and to not have it happen is a hurt that I cannot even begin to process. What I need from you, Dad, and what every kid needs from every parent is empathy. I know it is not the end of the world, but right now it feels like it is. So support me as I go through this, but know that this is a 'me' problem that I need to solve – not you. I need to let myself grieve, I need you to be present

and I need you to give me space, and confusing as that may sound to you, it makes perfect sense to me."

My kid said all that and a whole lot more, and we sat, and there were tears shed, and much as I wanted to fill the moment with words, I think the most important thing I did was to say nothing. There is a reason tradition teaches that when visiting a mourner during shiva, you are supposed to say nothing, rather to wait until the mourner speaks to you. Loss is best acknowledged with tears, with hugs, and with silence – not necessarily with words. It is not one size fits all, but let your polestar be your very presence, your honesty, your empathy, and most of all, your compassion.

The rebbe of the Warsaw Ghetto, Kalonymous Kalman Shapira, when asked by his community for a response to their suffering, at first suggested that perhaps it was an expression of God's will, a punishment perhaps, or maybe a test to strengthen their fortitude. But as suffering increased, Shapira's explanation changed. He wrote that at a moment of great suffering, God weeps for our suffering as we, a suffering humanity, weep with God. We weep together and are strengthened; we are broken but find the courage to go on. In the very moment that God seems most distant, God is right there next to us – weeping alongside us, supporting us, wiping away our tears. Maybe the proper and best response to a dream deferred is to perform the Godlike act of being present, affirming a person's pain, and standing by so that person can put one foot ahead of the other and then the other until they can support themselves.

Beginning with Adam and Eve being cast out of the Garden, the story of humanity is a tale of individuals seeking to reconstitute themselves in the face of setback and loss. Abraham and Sarah – barren; Isaac – scarred for life on Mount Moriah; Jacob – pitted from birth against his brother; Joseph – brought low being thrown into the pit. The list goes on and on and on. The story of Ruth, the hero of our coming harvest holiday, begins by defining Ruth as a widow – a dream deferred if there ever was one. Her story is one of rebuilding after the rug is ripped out from under her. We know that our present losses are an extension of that ongoing human drama, but that knowledge does not soften our sorrow. Like those who came before us, we stand outside the Garden, bound on the altar, thrown in the pit, our dreams deferred. And from the depths – *mima·amakim keratikha Yah* – we call out to God. We call out and we seek the divine presence of God and Godlike friends and family who acknowledge our pain, sitting there at our side, weeping as we weep, ready when we are ready to take a step forward.

May 9, 2020
15 Iyyar 5780

B'har/Beḥukkotai
Seminary Shabbat
From Chancellor to Chancellor

Of all the stories about Park Avenue Synagogue's relationship with the Jewish Theological Seminary, my favorite occurred in 1945 during the tenure of my predecessor twice-removed Rabbi Milton Steinberg, *z"l*. The then-president of the Seminary, Louis Finkelstein, understood JTS and, for that matter, Judaism as whole to have a universal mission: to be, in his words, "a civilizing influence on the modern world." (Michael B. Greenbaum, "The Finkelstein Era" in *Tradition Renewed: A History of The Jewish Theological Seminary of America*, ed. Jack Wertheimer, v1, p. 176) Grand as Finkelstein's vision was, it also meant that his views on Zionism were lukewarm at best. Despite his love for the Jewish people and even spiritual Zionism, Finkelstein could never quite square the circle of a Jewish nation-state. Having come of age during the Great War, he bristled against nationalisms of all kind; as the head of the leading Jewish educational institution of America, his bets were on Jewish life in the diaspora, not Palestine; as a human rights advocate, he would only support a Jewish state that conferred equal status to Christians and Muslims; not to mention that Finkelstein's fundraising base was dependent on Arthur Hayes Sulzberger and Lewis Strauss – two anti-Zionist JTS board members. Thus, despite the sentiment of most American Jews, the rabbinical leadership of the Conservative Movement, and the student body of the Seminary itself, Finkelstein stayed firm in his non-Zionism, going so far as to deny the request of the class of 1945 to sing *Hatikvah* at their commencement.

Park Avenue Synagogue's Rabbi Steinberg, an ardent Zionist who was then at the height of his national profile, would have none of it. He labeled the actions of Finkelstein's non-Zionist associates "'an expression of the most dejudaized and detraditionalized elements in American Jewish life' that fed into the hands of the anti-Zionist." (Naomi W. Cohen, "'Diaspora plus Palestine, Religion plus Nationalism': The Seminary and Zionism, 1902–1948" in *Tradition Renewed*, v.2, p. 156) Publicly and privately, Steinberg railed against Finkelstein's unenthusiastic support for a Jewish state, stating "I want Dr. Finkelstein . . . to stop pussyfooting on Zionism." (p. 162) In 1945, Steinberg, together with Rabbi Solomon Goldman, prepared a long list of grievances against Finkelstein, with Finkelstein's non-Zionism implicit in his list of complaints. So aggrieved was Steinberg in 1945 that he did the unthinkable, cancelling the annual Park Avenue Synagogue appeal for JTS and, lest there be any doubt, giving three public sermons questioning Finkelstein's power while lashing out at the JTS board as men "who are anti-traditionalist, anti-Zionist, even assimilationist" and "flagrantly out of harmony with everything the Seminary represents." (p. 162) By 1948, with the establishment of the State of Israel, any lingering non-Zionism on Finkelstein's part had become a moot point: by 1952, Finkelstein was awarding an honorary doctorate to Prime Minister Ben-Gurion. Looking back though, the Steinberg/Finkelstein, PAS/JTS exchange on Zionism serves as fascinating snapshot of profound transformations in American Jewish life.

Happy Seminary Shabbat! It is exactly seventy-five years since that dramatic exchange and not even COVID-19 can stop us from our annual Shabbat publicly affirming the Park Avenue Synagogue bond to JTS, where I was trained, where so many of our clergy and educators were trained, the institution to which we all owe so much. Last night we heard from Chancellor Arnold Eisen; tomorrow morning our community will be in Zoom dialogue with Chancellor Eisen on the future of synagogue life; and later this week, you will receive a link in our weekly email asking you to continue your support of JTS.

But this year is not just any year for JTS and PAS. This year is significant because next week will be the final commencement under Chancellor Eisen, who is retiring on June 30 after fourteen years of leadership. I have no idea who the next chancellor will be. The announcement, I imagine, will come after graduation by way of a plume of white smoke. This morning, in honor of the Chancellor and in honor of the Seminary, I invite you to take a stroll through history with me, the Seminary, and its leadership, a history that you will come to realize is altogether relevant for our present moment and shared future.

Our story begins with the founding of the Seminary in 1886, a time when Reform German Jewish leaders held sway over American Jewry and the masses of Eastern European Jews had just begun to arrive. In July of 1883, the Reform Movement celebrated the ordination of its graduating class with a meal that included clams, crabs, frog legs, and ice cream, a meal that – whether due to intent or oversight – signaled Reform's disdain for traditional Jewish observance. The "Treifah Banquet" combined with the movement's Pittsburgh platform, which boldly rejected Mosaic law, catalyzed a group of traditionalists to break away and create the Jewish Theological Seminary under its first leader, Rabbi Sabato Morais – a more traditional or conservative response to Reform. The arrival of millions of Eastern European Jews only intensified the rationale for a training ground for a modern, American, and traditional rabbinate.

After a decade and a half, recognizing the need for inspired leadership, JTS recruited the Romanian-born Solomon Schechter, the greatest English-speaking scholar of his day, made famous through his work on the Cairo Genizah. The combination of Schechter's vast rabbinic learning, secular training, and traditional orientation made him the perfect man for the time. Schechter's seminary was not only a bulwark against Reform, but an institution meant to train rabbis who could serve the Americanizing children of immigrants. As Schechter himself once quipped, for a rabbi to be successful in America, he must be able to speak baseball. Schechter never sought to create a new denomination. He had a broad vision of American Jewry, a shared middle ground: what he called Catholic Israel. Nevertheless, by the time Schechter died in 1915, he had not only assembled a world-class faculty of Jewish scholars, he had seeded the organizations – the United Synagogue, the Rabbinical Assembly – that would become the arms of what we now know as the Conservative Movement.

Cyrus Adler, the man who led the Seminary from Schechter's death until 1940, was as significant for what he was not as for what he was. He was not a rabbi; he was not a Jewish scholar; he was not a movement ideologue; and he was not, by all accounts, terribly charismatic. A bit like the biblical Isaac sandwiched between his visionary father Abraham and his tribe-producing son Jacob, Adler is often remembered as the guy between Schechter and Finkelstein. But like the biblical Isaac, Adler was the leader without whom JTS would have never survived: in the words of Mordecai Waxman, "a civil servant par excellence of American Jewish life." Adler led multiple institutions, edited numerous publications, and sat on the boards of every major Jewish organization. Remember, every legacy American Jewish organization you know – AJC, JDC, ADL, USCJ – was founded during these years. Adler brought them together and put JTS at the center. He also, probably most significantly, led JTS during the First World War, the financial crisis, and the depression, maintaining financial stability. For all of Schechter's gifts, an administrator he was not. Under Adler's watch, the Teacher's Institute was established, JTS graduates seeded Jewish communities nationwide, and JTS defined the "Position of the Seminary" between Reform and Orthodoxy. (Ira Robinson, "Cyrus Adler: President of the Jewish Theological Seminary 1915–1940" in *Tradition Renewed*, v.1, pp. 122–131)

Adler's successor, Louis Finkelstein, achieved national prominence beyond that of any other JTS chancellor. Throughout its history and to this day, JTS has squirmed on the question of whether it is the denominational fountainhead of the Conservative Movement or an institution in service to all of American Jewry. In Finkelstein's mind, the work of JTS was decidedly the latter: a center of teaching, research, and mass education. (Greenbaum, *Tradition Renewed*, p. 174) Camp Ramah, the Jewish Museum, and the west coast University of Judaism were all established during Finkelstein's tenure, as JTS strove to be *the* institution of higher Jewish learning in America and *the* representative of American Jewry. Finkelstein created the Eternal Light radio and television programs aimed to explain not just Judaism, but religion itself to America. Finkelstein was on the cover of *Time* magazine. Finkelstein created the Institute for Religious & Social Studies and the Lehmann Institute of Ethics, convened the Conference on Science, Philosophy and Religion, and so much more – all efforts to transcend boundaries of faith, denomination, and academic discipline. Finkelstein's efforts did not come without criticism – think of his aforementioned non-Zionism and his cool relationship with the Rabbinical Assembly; it was said that he had warmer relationships with non-Jews than with Conservative rabbis. And an Adler Finkelstein was not: For all his manifold gifts, Finkelstein's administrative shortcomings left JTS under profound financial distress.

The tenure of Finkelstein's successor, Gerson Cohen, was cut short for reasons of poor health. Cohen was a historian of first rank and, in my estimation, the most elegant expositor of all JTS chancellors. An academic at heart, Cohen deepened the community of Seminary scholarship, establishing doctoral programs and a graduate school now named in honor of our own Gershon Kekst, of blessed memory. Cohen created relationships with Columbia, Bank Street, Union Theological Seminary, and Princeton to name but a few. With the guidance and support of then PAS president Arthur Bienenstock, Cohen built the JTS library complex. In contrast to his predecessor, Cohen's Zionism was unflinching. He advocated on behalf of Masorti, the Conservative Movement in Israel, and set in motion the requirement for every rabbinical student to study in Jerusalem for a year. Of all of Cohen's achievements, he is perhaps remembered most as the chancellor under whose tenure women were first ordained rabbis, a decision for which he and our own Rabbi Judah Nadich, a member of the JTS board, advocated. (Paula E. Hyman "The Unfinished Symphony: The Gerson Cohen Years," in *Renewed Tradition*, v.1, pp. 233–268)

It is a little tricky for me to speak about Ismar Schorsch, the sixth JTS chancellor. He was my chancellor: I studied under him, and, truth be told, I am so very fond of him that it is difficult to be objective. A scholar of first rank who continues to publish to this day, Chancellor Schorsch, together with Park Avenue Synagogue's Gershon Kekst, led JTS for some twenty years through a time of heady expansion, turning JTS into a full-fledged university in its finances, faculty, student body, and otherwise. Schorsch founded and funded the Davidson Graduate School of Jewish Education. Schorsch sought to expand the mission of JTS well beyond Manhattan, expanding JTS's footprint in Israel and, as the Iron Curtain fell, creating Project Judaica, a Moscow-based program aimed at cultivating Russian Jewish leadership. In my mind, Schorsch represents the ideal of the scholar-mensch: a human being of profound depth and abiding kindness, pushing his students, myself included, to think deeply, passionately, and rigorously for ourselves and for the benefit of the Jewish communities we serve.

If it is difficult to assess Schorsch, then it is all the more awkward to speak about Chancellor Eisen before his tenure even concludes. What you should know is that aside from being a great scholar and a heck of a good guy, before becoming chancellor, Eisen published a book called *The Jew Within*, in which he explored the rise of "the sovereign self," a post-modern turn to a Jewish identity that prizes individualism and personal autonomy. Unlike Schechter, who had to educate immigrant Jews about America, or Finkelstein, who sought to explain Judaism to non-Jews, Eisen understood the task of JTS to be to train leaders to serve an American Jewry in search of personal meaning, for whom denominational lines matter less in an age of disintermediation, iPhones, and Amazon. It is not surprising that under Eisen's tenure, the JTS budget shifted from its graduate schools to its professional schools, including the establishment of a center for clinical pastoral education, a center for spiritual arts, and a center for ethics and justice. Eisen is leaving not just with a new building built, but with his fingerprints all over an institution aimed at developing leaders capable of serving the evolving spiritual needs of what Eisen calls the "vital Jewish center."

If, as Emerson once wrote, "Every great institution is the lengthened shadow of a single man," then in the case of JTS, it is an institution that can be understood in relation to the seven men (and they have all been men) who have led it. From the immigrant experience to the process of acculturation to the establishment of Israel to postwar suburbanization and upward mobility, to the age of the sovereign self, each leader has reflected and responded to the spirit of his age. It is not all neat and tidy, and I have omitted a lot, including the cantorial school, the library, the lay leaders, and of course the wider ecosystem of Jewish seminaries in America and Israel in which JTS functions. If nothing else though, it is useful and intriguing to track the chapters of the American Jewish experience through the chancellors of JTS.

Which begs the question: If every chancellor is a reflection of a particular chapter of American Jewish history, then what can we expect for the next chapter? Sometimes, social transformations can be seen only retrospectively through the eyes of history, and sometimes – as with the fifty-year jubilee intervals described in this week's Torah reading – they are marked by the passage of time. Right now, a social transformation is kicking down our front door as we are living through the unanticipated and unwelcome game changer of a global pandemic that I believe will upend everything, a subset of "everything" being American Jewry. How communities are created and sustained, how education takes shape, how identity itself is formed – all is being accelerated; every assumption is up for grabs in a jubilee we didn't want or ask for, in which the past is not at all an indicator of the future.

And . . . there is about to be a new chancellor. A chancellor who will have to guide JTS through this *midbar*, this wilderness that he or she presumably did not even know about when applying for the job. A chancellor who, like every chancellor, will have to train rabbis, cantors, educators and scholars capable of leading an American Jewry and America in desperate need of moral leadership. An American Jewry that is transforming tradition in real time, as evidenced by the livestream you are watching. An American Jewry in search of the theological language capable of voicing the searching questions of our age. In all the tumult, I take comfort in the knowledge that these tasks of leadership development, theological inquiry, and balancing tradition and change are the very efforts, the bread and butter, that has guided JTS since its inception.

All of which brings us back to where we began. No matter the chapter of JTS history, the membership of Park Avenue Synagogue has always been at its side. When JTS needed to be pushed – on Zionism, on feminism – we have pushed as an ally, Her Majesty's loyal opposition, if you will. Our rabbis and lay leadership have been JTS board leadership and chairmen: Gershon Kekst, of blessed memory, and the present chairman, our own PAS past chairman Allen Levine. On occasion we have used the power of the purse as a stick, but far more frequently we have been the ones to seed initiatives, fund scholarships, and, when needed, build buildings. In every chapter, under every chancellor, the abiding support of our community for JTS has been the constant because we at PAS know that the rabbis, cantors, educators, and scholars of JTS serve not just the future of our synagogue, but the future of American Jewry. In all the unknowns of the present, I am so very excited to think about this time next year, when the new chancellor of JTS visits Park Avenue Synagogue and we welcome him or her warmly, the PAS-JTS bond closer than ever. *Ḥazak, ḥazak v'nit'ḥazek*. Let us be strong, be strong, and let us be strengthened.

May 16, 2020
22 Iyyar 5780

Shavuot, Yizkor
Together . . . Apart

Long before its present usage, those who come to synagogue to recite Yizkor on Yom Kippur, Sukkot, Pesach, and today – Shavuot – have well understood the meaning of the expression "together apart." At Yizkor, young and old, synagogue regulars alongside more infrequent attendees, some coming for the first time and others for longer than we can remember – all arrive for a moment of intentional memory. This one remembering a brother, that one a spouse, this one a child, that one a mother – some loved ones having suffered tragic deaths while others were granted length of years. To a rabbi, there is a differentiated and palpable feeling to a Yizkor room; everyone present shares the fact of loss – but every loss is unique. Together and apart – all at the same time. This year, the fact of our physical "apart-ness" only amplifies this Yizkor feeling. We are deprived of our Sanctuary, we are physically distant from one another, *and* we are joined together in our remembrances of our loved ones.

In loss, "together apart." This morning we read the book of Ruth and I imagine that is exactly how Ruth and Naomi felt on their journey to Bethlehem. The back story, we know, is one of natural catastrophe: a famine resulting in geographic displacement and economic insecurity. Seeking to improve their lot, Naomi and her husband Elimelech travelled to Moab, where their sons Mahlon and Chilion married two local Moabite women, Ruth and Orpah respectively. By the fourth verse of the book, Elimelech has passed. By the following verse, so have Naomi's two sons. Returning home, Naomi is bereft of everything save one of her foreign-born daughters-in-law. "Do not call me Naomi, meaning 'pleasant,'" she tells her neighbors; "Call me Mara, meaning 'bitter.' . . . I went away full and have returned empty." Naomi's loss is incalculable: her husband, her sons – a heartache beyond measure – a heartache all her own.

But Naomi was not the only one on that journey to Bethlehem who had suffered loss. Ruth was widowed as well, her love Mahlon taken before his time. One could, I suppose, say that at least Ruth did not lose a child and she, unlike Naomi, had youth on her side; she could begin again. And yet to a certain degree, Ruth's sense of loss exceeded that of Naomi. Naomi, after all, could return home to her people. Having married into an Israelite household, Ruth had presumably severed her ties to her Moabite family. Ruth's decision to bind her destiny to Naomi and the God of Israel make her the gold standard for all future converts, but lest we forget, it also served a practical purpose: Ruth had nowhere else to go. Naomi and Ruth were two widows journeying together to Bethlehem; they were together apart, their sorrows particular to each of them.

And it wasn't just Ruth and Naomi. There is a third widow, or widower, in our story: Boaz. The Talmud explains that Boaz has also suffered the loss of his beloved, going so far as to suggest that on the very day that Naomi and Ruth arrived in Bethlehem, Boaz had just buried his wife. Boaz may have been blessed with material comfort, but as he was aging and without an heir, his legacy was altogether uncertain. Were there to have been a Yizkor service in Bethlehem, I have no doubt that sitting there in the pews would have been Naomi, Ruth, Boaz, and so many others – together apart, tears flowing freely – each recalling their respective loved ones. And each reflecting on the uncertainty of their present and future.

The redemptive arc of the book of Ruth is not linear. Neither Ruth nor Naomi nor Boaz regain their fullness all at once. The comfort each of them seeks comes by virtue of individual acts of goodness, kindness, and compassion, retrieved, like the barley harvest, one sheaf at a time. The first, and perhaps most famous act of *hesed*, is Ruth's initial kindness to Naomi: "Your people will be my people, where you go, I will go . . . ." Ruth understands that however she and her mother-in-law differed in age, origin, and otherwise, as widows, the two of them share far more, and in her understanding, Ruth looks beyond her loss to comfort Naomi.

Ruth's act of *hesed*, kindness, is repaid on that fateful day when, once in Israel, she goes out to glean in what turns out to be Boaz's field. Boaz is impressed with Ruth and with what he has heard of her kindness to Naomi. He offers Ruth both blessing and protection as she gleans. Boaz has nothing to gain; his is a straightforward act of kindness and a mirror into Boaz's soul. No matter the inner grief that he was experiencing, Boaz did not lose the ability to look outward and offer a helping hand to this young foreign woman.

The combination of Ruth's industriousness and Boaz's responsiveness prompts Naomi to set aside her all-consuming and self-declared bitterness and consider something that people in pain usually don't see: a future. Naomi devises a plan to find a home for Ruth, not a simple task for her in that it involves finding a mate for her dead son's widow, a task undoubtedly laden with all sorts of emotions. And yet she does exactly that. Like Ruth to Naomi, like Boaz to Ruth, Naomi breaks through the shell of her own sorrows in order to perform a grand act of kindness toward another.

And then, at night on the threshing floor, Ruth courageously presses beyond her comfort zone, reciprocating kindness to Boaz. "Blessed be the Lord," Boaz tells Ruth, "your latest deed of kindness is greater than the first, in that you have not turned to younger men, whether poor or rich." Boaz knows full well that Ruth has options; presumably Ruth knows, too. But Boaz is kin to Naomi by way of her late husband. I learned from my colleague Rabbi Eli Kaunfer this past week, that in the Middle Ages when a widow and a widower married, instead of the traditional seven wedding blessings mentioning Adam and Eve, an alternative blessing was substituted that referenced Boaz and Ruth. The love of Ruth and Boaz represents the possibility of love emerging following loss. Ruth and Boaz's love signals what happens when two people recognize that despite loss, a person can extend an act of kindness and help lessen the loss of another.

Ruth to Naomi, Naomi to Ruth, Ruth to Boaz, and the community bearing witness to it all. Kindness begetting kindness, goodness generating further goodness. The power of the book of Ruth is that a virtuous cycle is created in which the emptiness of each character is "filled" by way of good deeds extended one to another. Lest we forget, the name Ruth has the same etymology as the word meaning "to fill," as the cantor just chanted in the twenty-third psalm: *Kosi r'vaya*, my cup overflows. Ruth, both the book and the person, teach us that however aching our emptiness, it can be filled. No matter how empty we are, we can and perhaps must fill each other's emptiness. We can fill each other up.

Let this be our charge this year in this Yizkor hour. In this holiday of first fruits, the baskets of our harvest are filled with the bounty of memory. We recall the kindnesses of those who came before us: their compassion, their wisdom, their sacrifice, and most of all their love. As we reflect on their lives, we are grateful, and we are filled with sadness at their loss – fullness and emptiness at the same time. It is important to be present in our sorrow, failing to do so would ignore not only the humanity of the person we mourn but our own humanity as well. And yet, we have learned from Ruth that we can assign meaning to the lives of our loved ones – and our own – by filling our days with acts of *hesed*, kindness. No matter the depth of our sorrow, none of us is emptyhanded; we can give of the fruits of our own good deeds – freely, selflessly, and compassionately. No differently than a person, no matter their financial straits, is still obligated by Jewish law to give a token of *tzedakah*; so too a person, no matter their grief, should not abstain from the opportunity and obligation to ease the grief and pain of another person.

Together apart. This is who we are, this Yizkor, this Shavuot, this year, but really, always. Such is the limitation of being human: our joys, our sorrows, our lives understood by us and us alone. The holes left by the loss of our loved ones have only set us apart further. We feel our emptiness deeply. We cannot wish it away. So let us respond as did Ruth, as did Naomi, as did Boaz, as did our loved ones before us.

Those whom we remember today, they too knew loss, and yet they nevertheless filled our lives with love. With acts of *hesed* one to the other to the other, let us fill each other up, from futility to fulfillment, from emptiness to overflow, the tears that are sown today to be reaped one day with joy.

May 30, 2020
7 Sivan 5780

Naso
That's My Bible

Of all the thoughts that ran through my mind Monday evening as I watched President Trump stand in front of Washington, DC's historic St. John's Episcopal Church, Bible in hand, the one I want to talk to you about today does not concern the forcible removal of protesters for the photo op, nor the fact that neither the president nor any of his aides were practicing safe social distancing, nor the reporter's question as to whether it was the president's own Bible. That evening, we were – as we remain today – in the midst of a national crisis. A double pandemic: COVID-19 and the virus of systemic racism, the latter's latest victim, George Floyd, murdered on the evening of May 25 when a white police officer pressed his knee to Floyd's neck for almost nine minutes. In city after city across the country, protests have burst onto the streets in grief and anger over the killing of Floyd and in recognition that his death was emblematic of a legacy of pain, of injustice extending back hundreds of years and deep into the fault lines of our nation's soul. It was a moment that called for leadership, for clarity of message, for perspective, and for action, and in the president's hand was the best, oldest, most sacred, and most effective tool of communication known to humanity: the Bible. God's honest truth. As the president stood in front of St. John's, I thought to myself, *Hey, he's holding a Bible. I am a rabbi; I know that book! That's my book!*

It wasn't a terribly deep thought, but it led me to my next, slightly deeper thought. "With the world on fire," I wondered to myself, "what biblical verse, what chapter, what narrative does the nation need to hear at this moment? What passage could the president draw from for inspiration? Had I been standing there whispering into the president's ear (socially distanced, of course), what would I have told the president to read?

Now, not everyone knows the Bible like rabbis do, but most everyone has heard the Creation story. So my first instinct might be to suggest starting at the very beginning (a very good place to start), Genesis 1:27. "And God created humanity in the divine image, in the image of God humanity was created, male and female God created them." It is arguably the first statement and founding principle of all of biblical theology: the belief that every human being contains the divine image within and is therefore to be accorded equal and infinite dignity. Young and old, rich and poor, whatever your gender, whatever your sexual orientation, certainly whatever the color of your skin – we are all equal and we all deserve respect. It this principle that binds us together in all our diversity – the thread, the connective tissue that runs from Genesis to the final chapters of the Prophets. As is written in Malachi: "Do we not all have one father? Did not one God create us?" (2:10) The second chapter of Genesis explains that when God created the first person, God blew the breath of life into him – the human *neshamah*, the divine human soul. When George Floyd was murdered, when he uttered those desperate words "I can't breathe," it was the last gasp of his breath of life, his divine soul being destroyed. The souls of George Floyd, of Ahmaud Arbery, of Breonna Taylor, of Eric Garner, of Amadou Diallo, and of countless other peopl of color. To hold the Bible is to hold human life sacred, and to destroy one life is to destroy an entire world. If I had to quote from scripture Monday night, Genesis chapter one would be the obvious, dare I say, easiest place to start.

Some may say the job of the president is not to be a theologian, but a comforter in chief. Fair enough. Maybe in this uncertain, unsettling, and grief-stricken time, our country needed the rhetoric of comfort. Think of President Reagan following the Challenger, President Bush following 9/11, and President Obama at the memorial site years later. "The Lord is our refuge and strength, our help in times of trouble." It was understood that President Obama chose Psalm 46 as an allusion to 8:46 am, the time the hijacked jet hit the North Tower. Ironically the current president could have used the same psalm this past Monday, for the eight minutes and forty-six seconds that the police officer's knee was on George Floyd's neck. Psalms of comfort remind us that the Lord is near the broken-hearted. (Psalm 34) They give voice to the hope that though we may lie down at night with tears, joy will come in the morning. (Psalm 30) Biblical psalms also give expression to our rage, asking why the innocent suffer, why the wicked prosper, and why the world – good as it is – is so very far from perfect. "How long, O Lord, will you hide your face?" (Psalm 13) "How long will you show favor to the wicked? (Psalm 82) Reading a psalm of comfort or one of lament doesn't lessen your pain. But it does make you feel less alone in your pain: Someone else has walked this dark path. The Psalms offer the sacred vocabulary for what we are feeling – a rod and a staff to hold us up. When in pain, when seeking comfort, reach for the book of Psalms. It is always a solid bet to read and, if need be, to quote.

I have to imagine that on Monday night, the thought on many Americans' minds, certainly on my mind, was the uncomfortable question of "How am I a contributor to racism, what is my responsibility, and what should be my response?" This is actually the very first question of the Bible: "Where are you?" God asks Adam. "Where is your brother?" God demands of Cain. "Your brother's blood cries out to Me from the ground." A teacher of mine once taught that the entirety of Jewish ethics is a rejoinder to Cain's question "Am I my brother's keeper?" We are our brothers' and our sisters' keepers. We dare not shrug our shoulders. We dare not be complicit, well-meaning collaborators and enablers perpetuating a system of racial injustice. It is not enough just to be not-racist; we need to be anti-racist. Leviticus (19:18) teaches that we are obligated to love our neighbors as ourselves. And that obligation, that empathy for one another, has nothing to do with whether the other shares our neighborhood, nationality, or shade of skin. Moses himself, from the comfort of Pharaoh's palace, witnessed a Hebrew slave being struck by the Egyptian taskmaster. He heard the cry, he looked here and there, and he realized two things. First, that he shared a bond of kinship with the man being beaten; and second, that if he didn't take action, nobody would. This is the calling card of the Bible – to remember that you yourself were once a stranger in a strange land and so you must always heed the cry of the oppressed and respond. Whether that person looks like you, prays like you, or speaks like you, that person is your kin, and your empathy and action must be extended to that person.

Sometimes, the Bible is there to challenge us, and if nothing else, this week has been a challenging one to sort out. Monday night was a confusing night. Yes, there were peaceful protests, but there was also looting on the streets of Manhattan. I couldn't sleep Monday night – for many reasons, of which one was my concern whether the physical structure of the synagogue was safe. What is the difference between a just protestor and a hoodlum? What is the line between a good cop and a bad cop? To what degree is one generation obligated to right the wrongs of past generations? These questions demand tough conversations – conversations that must allow for texture, not soundbites or shame-facing shouting matches. Here, too, the Bible can help. Isaiah knew there was a difference between good and evil when he preached, "I the Lord love justice; I hate robbery and wrong." (61:8) Proverbs made the same distinction: "Evil people do not understand justice, but those who seek the Lord understand it completely." (28:5) The book of Exodus states pretty clearly that children will be held accountable for the sins of their fathers. (20:5) The book of Ezekiel states the opposite just as clearly: "The righteousness of the righteous shall be upon himself, and the wickedness of the wicked shall be upon himself." (18:19-20)

It would have been a little highbrow for Monday evening, but imagine if the president had announced a national conversation on the subject "What does the Bible have to say about intergenerational sin?" Heck, I would have been satisfied had the president simply made reference to this week's Torah reading, which contains the fascinating question of the difference between sincere and insincere confession. The Bible understood that for any society to sustain itself, it has to make space for conversations about confession, accountability, forgiveness, and restorative justice. Come to think about it, this week's Torah reading would have been as good a text as any to voice all the thorny conversations our country needs to have.

As to the question of how societies house dissent, make course corrections, bend the moral arc toward justice – this is the backbone of prophetic literature. Moses standing before Pharaoh, the daughters of Zelophehad seeking justice as women, the prophet Nathan calling out the excesses of the monarchy in the court of King David – the Bible well understood that a just society comes only by way of an active give and take, checks and balances between the offices of priest, prophet, and king. "Justice, justice thou shalt pursue." (Deuteronomy 16:20) Why is the word "justice" repeated? Because justice must be pursued both when it is easy and when it is hard. "What is it that the Lord requires of you?" asks the prophet Micah. "To do justice, love kindness, and walk humbly before your God." (6:8) "Let justice roll down like waters," preached Amos, "and righteousness like an ever-flowing stream." (5:4) The words of the prophets were not spoken with the thought that one day they would be inscribed on marble memorials. They were spoken in the face of injustice, at great risk to the speaker, to be etched into the hearts of the listeners and acted upon. Isaiah, Jeremiah, Amos, Ezekiel – the entire second part of the Hebrew Bible, its core section, devoted to the prophetic call for justice in the face of those who would have it otherwise. What could have been quoted on Monday night? Pretty much anything from the books of the prophets.

In answer to the question of what verse could have been cited Monday night, truth be told, there is no end. Want to talk about the need for leadership? Quote the book of Esther. Want to talk about building bridges between historic enemies? Quote the book of Ruth. Want to talk about the need for national unity? Do what Lincoln did, and speak of a "house divided." Want to talk about the need for peace and civility? Remind us that "everyone shall sit under their vine and under their fig tree; and none shall make them afraid. (Micah 4:4) Courage? Take me to Daniel in the lion's den. Contrition? Take me to

Jonah in the belly of the whale. The consequence of a society that is all swagger and no substance? Teach me about Samson, the subject of today's haftarah. There was so much that sacred scripture could have taught us on Monday evening – to heal us, to challenge us, to prompt dialogue and action.

Sadly, we know that is not what happened. On Monday evening, the Bible remained shut – our most sacred text, held literally upside-down, turned into a cheap prop for political gain.

I am a rabbi and I know that book. That book is my book; that book is our book; that book is God's book. We dare not, we cannot, and I will not ever abdicate my right to speak in the name of our sacred texts, certainly not in a time of crisis and not when others are arrogating that right to themselves. That text is too sacred, the stakes are too high, and this country is too fragile to let people lay claim to a book who don't even know how to open it and use its power to bring healing to our country and our souls in such desperate need of repair.

June 6, 2020
14 Sivan 5780

Sh'laḥ L'kha
Speaking Privately

These past weeks, as our synagogue has embraced Pride Month and the Supreme Court has made a historic and heroic decision barring discrimination based on sexual orientation and gender identity, my thoughts turned to a more modest episode in the long, tortured, and ongoing fight to end legal discrimination against LGBTQ+ people.

The year was 2012 and the issue of the hour was same-sex marriage for all Americans, a right that at the time, you may recall, President Obama had stopped short of endorsing. On the morning of Sunday, May 6, Vice President Biden broached the issue on national television, telling NBC's "Meet the Press" that he was "absolutely comfortable with the fact that men marrying men, women marrying women, and heterosexual men and women marrying are entitled to the exact same rights, all the civil rights, all the civil liberties." Journalists pounced on the perceived daylight between Biden's and Biden's boss's evolving views on gay marriage, to the point that in the days ahead, Obama would reflect publicly that the vice president had "probably gotten a little bit over his skis." In the next few days the White House reported that Biden had apologized to Obama privately for his public verbal foot fault.

The most interesting thing about the entire episode, however, was neither Biden's misstep, nor Obama's "over his skis" turn of phrase, which has become part of the American lexicon, but the fact that despite what was reported, Biden never actually apologized for a verbal misfire. In fact, soon thereafter President Obama became a full-throated supporter of gay marriage, stating: "Our journey is not complete until our gay brothers and sisters are treated like anyone else under the law." It is worth pausing to appreciate the political theater of it all. Biden's public statement provided Obama with a trial balloon for a major policy shift. Obama's mild rebuke provided him with plausible deniability and political cover from the naysayers. While Biden's publicly (mis)reported private apology may have denied Obama the short-term advantage of a principled stance in favor of gay marriage, in the long run it arguably accomplished the task of bending the moral arc towards justice with the Supreme Court's ultimate 2015 decision on gay marriage. Change happened, and everybody, more or less, came out a winner. Was the entire series of events by design? Some sort of staged Kabuki dance? Only two people will ever know. What we do know is that the vignette serves as a case study in how the political game is played and how social change actually happens, specifically, how public pressure can be effectively leveraged to prompt individuals in power to bring about much-needed transformation.

If the Biden-Obama story stands as an example of the effective use of the public sphere, then this morning's Torah reading illustrates the pitfalls of using the public sphere poorly. At God's command, Moses sends twelve spies to scout out the land: to assess its inhabitants, its fruits, and its fortifications. The spies do as they are instructed and after forty days, return to Moses and the entire Israelite community. The land is beautiful, they say, but we cannot attack the inhabitants. They are stronger than we are; we looked like grasshoppers in their eyes and in our own. Joshua and Caleb try to counter the report of the ten other spies, but to no avail; the people's will has been broken. The Israelites will be punished with forty years of wandering in the desert, one year for each day of the scouts' mission, an entire generation deemed unworthy to enter the promised land.

Every year we read the story of the spies, and every year the reader is left with the gnawing question of "Why?" Why were the spies punished? They were told to scout out the land, come back, and deliver a report so Moses could proceed accordingly. They did what they were told; they agreed on what they saw; they came back and shared it. What precisely was their sin?

Some interpreters suggest that their failing was a lack of faith – in Moses, in God, and in themselves – their loss of nerve, their longing for Egypt, prompting them to create fake facts and mislead the people. Others have suggested that their sin was one of mishearing Moses's charge. Moses was not interested in the question of *whether* the land should be conquered; rather, Moses needed counsel on *how* to do it. The spies were stuck on the question of *whether*, while Moses had asked the question of *how* – a subtle but critical distinction in this story and so many others.

Compelling as these reasons and others may be, in my mind the fundamental misstep of the story boils down to the issue of the public vs. the private sphere. The text is specific: The spies shared their findings before the entire people of Israel. Once the spies publicly forced Moses's hand with news he neither anticipated nor desired, he did what any human being would do under such circumstances. Flatfooted and embarrassed publicly, he dug in his heels and swung back. The spies could have pulled Moses aside; they could have let him know, on the QT, that bad news was on the way. And Moses, I imagine, had he been extended that courtesy, could have caught his breath, regrouped, and recalibrated. But that is not what happened. Were we to stage this tale today, I would have the spies post their reports on their Facebook pages, and then spotlight Moses's reaction as he checked his account to discover that the feedback he had asked for was being reported not just to him, but to the entire world!

The spies failed on a number of levels, and Moses's hands are not entirely clean either; he could have handled himself differently. But it is the failure to appreciate the difference between feedback given privately and publicly that stands out to me as the damning failure of the spies and the entire wilderness generation. Their misstep is brought into focus by our haftarah, when, forty years later, the spies that Joshua sends out to Jericho report back to Joshua and only Joshua. This failure is the sin that ties together this entire section of the Torah.

Last week, Miriam and Aaron spoke out against Moses, a sin both in what they said and how they said it – publicly. So, too, next week, the challenge of Koraḥ and his company, a rebellion that, in rabbinic literature, becomes the paradigm for an unholy controversy. And the following week, when Moses is barred from entering the land for striking the rock, the punishment seems incommensurate with Moses's lapse in judgement until you realize that God's wrath was kindled not so much for the act of hitting the rock as for the fact that Moses did so publicly, before all of Israel. Even, and perhaps especially, God knows the difference between the public and private sphere. Each one of these stories, as well as others I have not mentioned, would have turned out differently had the involved parties simply paused two beats to consider not just what they were going to say or do, but how and in whose company they were going to make their opinions and actions known.

Ours is a charged season with no shortage of pressing social and political issues. Some days – actually most days – I feel like the man in the old story who complains to his rabbi that his house is too crowded, and the rabbi instructs him to bring chickens, then a cow, then visiting relatives into his home. We have a pandemic; we have economic uncertainty; we have racial strife; we have an imminent annexation of the West Bank; we have a crisis in the attorney general's office; we have antisemitism on the left and right. Rabbi, my house is full! We are all wondering what we can do, how we can effect change, how we can move the needle a little bit, do our part to make this broken world a little less broken.

In our desire to right the wrongs and heal the world, we want to call out injustice, foot faults, and sins small and large; we dare not stay silent. Those of us who know our history know that neither individuals nor societies change from a place of comfort. Inspirational "ask not" speeches are nice, but generally speaking, fireside chats and stirring appeals to our better angels do not prompt perpetrators of wrongdoing to mend their wicked ways. Think of any movement of social change, from Moses to MLK to Harvey Milk and everyone in between. At some point there had to be public pressure; at some point, someone had to be forced to do something that would not have come about otherwise owing to simple inertia. What were the ten plagues if not a public demonstration of God's might to bend the will of Pharaoh before the Egyptian public? As Jews, we of all people know the price of public silence. How much human savagery, the Shoah included, could have been limited, if only the press, public officials, and the general public had been more forceful in their denouncements. Thank God, thank God, the framers of the Bill of Rights, with the Boston Massacre still fresh in their mind, chose to protect "the right of the people peaceably to assemble, and to petition the government for a redress of grievances." For us as Americans, as Jews, and as lovers of Israel, there is a time – and that time is now – that we not only *can* speak up, but we *must* speak up. Sometimes people need to be forced to do the right thing.

And we need to use our heads. Because as much as I fear for the health of our society, as much as I believe in the power of public speech and the press as instruments of change, I also fear for the well-being of so many whose humanity is forever diminished by our contemporary call-out culture. If we see something, we should say something. But lately, it seems that rather than seeking understanding, dialogue, and change, we have become satisfied with publicly shaming individuals before the facts are in, before the context is understood, before we have extended to others the same courtesy we would ask for ourselves when our actions come under fire. To defame another person by way of social media is not dialogic and it does not make you an instrument of social change; it is a way to seek cheap high fives from your own teammates. It prompts the other party to dig in his or her heels, because like Moses, we all respond differently to feedback when it is delivered publicly. Denouncing someone on social media also undercuts the possibility of rehabilitating a relationship when the offending incident has passed. It is a moral failing akin to that of the spies. It is easy, really easy, just to hit "reply all," forward someone's private email, post what you heard third-hand on Twitter as fact, call someone out, cancel someone's communal standing, crush a person's future by way of your self-declared moral certitude and the echo chamber of your Facebook friends. You know what takes courage? You know what takes character? To pick up a phone. To seek to understand and to be understood. Those ten plagues God inflicted on Egypt – they only happened after Pharaoh stonewalled Moses's repeated entreaties to let his people go. Tradition teaches that a person's good name, *shem tov*, is our most valuable asset. At risk of stating the obvious, in a social media age we are all stakeholders in maintaining the share value of each other's reputations.

No more than forty-eight hours ago, I phoned a congregant, a kind and wise and long-standing member of the community. After a bit of a catch-up, he paused, began to open up, and shared with me that he was glad we were talking, because I had, some time ago, caused him hurt. It was an honest conversation, and together we unpacked the incident in question. He understood that I meant no ill will, and upon my apology, he forgave freely and lovingly. When I put down the phone, aside from being totally mortified at the thought that I had caused him hurt, I was grateful. I realized what I had done; I understood how in that moment I could have been better; and while I can't undo the past, I am resolved to move forward intentionally, hopefully never to be so clumsy in my words or deeds. And you know why it went so well, what made the conversation possible and hopefully made me a better person? The conversation happened privately, in confidence, with a readiness to share hard truths and perhaps most importantly, a willingness to listen on both sides.

When Shabbat concludes tonight, I will say havdalah with my family as I do every week. When we say the third *brakhah*, we will raise our hands to the light of the candle. There are many explanations why we do this, and one, taught to me as a young child, is to remind us that to shame another person in public is akin to the crime of murder, *sh'fikhut damim*, the spilling of blood. To damage a person's reputation is like taking their life. Why do we lift up our hands to the candle? In order to examine our fingers and check if there is blood on our hands owing to the sin of careless speech. Always, but especially in this time when we are all physically isolated from another, let's make sure our hands are clean. Let's presume positive intent and do each other the courtesy of picking up a phone.

Shabbat is a time to imagine the world not as it is, but as it should be. This Shabbat perhaps more than most, we are all scouting out what the future holds, wondering what we can do and say and protest to close that gap by getting involved and speaking out – in New York, across our country, and in Israel. Sometimes we need to shout loudly; sometimes we need to hold our tongue; and sometimes we need to think tactically, to get over our skis with the aim of prompting other people to head where they need to go – with their reputations intact. The gift of speech can change the world; it can also destroy it. This Shabbat let us remember that it is in our power to choose our words carefully, to determine to whom they are spoken and where they are posted. Doing that we will arrive together – please God soon – in the promised land.

June 20, 2020
28 Sivan 5780

Pinḥas
First Base on Race

First base may not be the most obvious place to begin a sermon on race, but in honor of the soon-to-begin baseball season, I will take my lead from there.

The baserunner that 1947 day in May was Hank Greenberg. It was the final season for the legendary slugger who hit fifty-eight home runs in 1938, the ballplayer who achieved mythical status in the Jewish imagination for his decision not to play when a pennant game fell on Yom Kippur in 1934. Celebrated though he was by the Jewish community, Greenberg had been subjected throughout his career to antisemitic taunts from opposing players and fans. These were the years of Charles Lindbergh, Father Coughlin, and Henry Ford, of implicit and explicit antisemitism, when Roosevelt's New Deal was referred to as the "Jew Deal," when hotel signs read "No dogs or Jews allowed," and when the word "Jew" was commonly hurled as an accepted insult. As a first baseman, stationed by the opposing team's dugout, Greenberg had been subjected to just about every antisemitic insult imaginable.

Playing first for the Brooklyn Dodgers that day was Jackie Robinson, the rookie ballplayer who had recently broken Major League Baseball's color line. The rattling that Robinson had received thus far was much worse than just racial slurs. Days earlier, Robinson's life had been threatened, and his family had received threats that his infant son Jackie Jr. would be kidnapped. Members of opposing teams sat in their dugouts pointing their bats at him and simulating machine gun noises. The Phillies coach fined his pitchers if they failed to throw at Robinson. The hotel where the Dodgers stayed refused to admit Robinson, and the organist at Cincinnati's Crosley Field played "Bye, Bye, Blackbird" as Robinson walked off the field. No wonder Robinson's batting average had slumped. No wonder he was contemplating quitting.

Early in the game, after laying down a perfect bunt, Robinson had collided with Greenberg at first, with Robinson going on to reach second. The following inning, Greenberg was walked. Arriving at first base, Greenberg asked Robinson if he had been hurt in the earlier collision, and Robinson assured Greenberg that he hadn't been. Greenberg then said to Robinson, "Don't pay any attention to these guys who are trying to make it hard for you. Stick in there. . . . I hope you and I can get together for a talk. There are a few things I've learned through the years that might help you and make it easier."

Robinson was deeply moved by Greenberg's supportive words and praised him in the African American press. Following the game, The *New York Times* reported Jackie saying, "Class tells. It sticks out all over Mr. Greenberg." The two men would always remain in touch, their meeting at first base becoming the foundation for their friendship for years ahead. (S. Harwood, H. Brackman, "Going to Bat for Jackie Robinson: The Jewish Role in Breaking Baseball's Color Line." *Journal of Sports History*, Spring 1999, pp. 115-141)

This morning, I want to use the image of Greenberg and Robinson together at first base to frame some preliminary reflections about race, reflections I believe to be both modest and ambitious. Neither Greenberg nor Robinson was a political philosopher, nor, for that matter, a community activist. They were athletes. As Mark Kurlansky explains in his book *Hank Greenberg: The Hero Who Didn't Want to Be One*, Greenberg had an ambivalent relationship with his Judaism; his dream was to be a great ballplayer, never a great *Jewish* ballplayer. Which is why, I think, I love the image of the two men that day in Pittsburgh. Standing at first base with Robinson at his side, Greenberg realized that there was a bit of his own story in Robinson's story. Greenberg didn't have to say anything. It was the final year of his career as a player, and because of the reserve clause, he had been ingloriously traded to the Pittsburgh Pirates. Greenberg would have been well within his rights to give Robinson a nod and carry on his business. But that is not what he did. He saw Robinson and acknowledged that he, perhaps better than anyone, understood the uphill battle

Robinson faced, and given the choice of doing nothing or doing something, he chose the latter, becoming what we would call an ally.

In the years ahead, Greenberg would leverage his stature more forcefully. As General Manager for the Cleveland Indians, Greenberg would be publicly criticized for fielding too many African Americans – more than any other team. As GM, Greenberg refused to have his team stay at any hotel that denied admittance to all his players, remembering when he, as a ballplayer, had been denied rooms at hotels because he was Jewish. Greenberg knew the structural racism that African American ballplayers faced, and in his spheres of influence, to the degree that he could, took steps to dismantle it. But Greenberg's activism did not begin when he was a GM. It began when he realized that his own words, his own actions, and his own behavior mattered – his willingness to respond to his inner compass and connect to the common humanity of another, no matter the color of their skin. That happened on first base that 1947 day.

"To think of man in terms of white, black, or yellow," wrote Rabbi Abraham Joshua Heschel, "is more than an error. It is an eye disease, a cancer of the soul." Heschel spoke those words at a 1963 Conference on race and religion, in a time that, like our own, sought redress against the systemic injustices experienced by the African American community. In calling out racism as an eye disease, Heschel signaled that important as the civil rights agenda was, the first step was to address the root cause of racism: the prejudices, biases, and chauvinisms that lie within the heart and soul of every human being. Similar to King's message later that year from his Birmingham jail cell, the object of Heschel's prophetic charge was not so much the overt racist, but rather the well-intended white person whose unexamined prejudices perpetuated the structural impediments to creating a just society.

Yes, there were public battles to be fought against segregation – sit-ins and freedom rides, marches and protests – but the segregation on Heschel's mind was between humanity and God. Heschel reminded his audience that the front line of the fight against racism was in one's soul, an impassioned plea that every human be treated with the honor due to a being created in the divine image. Yes, the laws on the books had to be changed, but that was a process contingent on every person examining their received biases and addressing their internalized prejudices. Then and only then could the systemic and enduring societal changes take place. Akin to how Brown v. Board of Education, the landmark 1954 case that overturned "separate-but-equal," was informed by doll tests revealing the pernicious effects of segregation on young children, Heschel knew that the root cause of the societal ills of his era could be found in the heart of every individual listening to his words. Some may have been more guilty than others, but everyone was a contributor, everyone was responsible.

And what Heschel understood then is as true today as it ever was. We could, if we so chose, talk about Black Lives Matter, police reform, the politics of monuments, intersectionality, and educational access. We could talk about all sorts of uncomfortable things, leaving some people to think we are saying too much and others that we are saying too little. But as the leader of a religious institution, it strikes me that my primary calling card is to prompt the really uncomfortable conversation lived by each of us regarding the degree to which we do or don't see our fellow as created equally in the image of God. To ask ourselves the awkward question of implicit bias, the manner in which we have been conditioned to see the world, to see "the other," and consider if the lens of our vision, and by extension of our souls, is not more distorted than we would care to admit.

Most of us, I hope, do not consider ourselves to be racist. Most of us, I imagine, would say of ourselves that we give everyone a fair shake, treat everyone the same way, judge people by their character, not the color of their skin. Further, some would say, we give to the right causes, supporting scholarships and assistance to those seeking educational and economic access. We are, after all, a socially liberal New York synagogue. We are the good guys. If we cannot be relied on as allies, then who? But then I catch myself as I walk into a store, realizing that I have already made a million assumptions about who does what – based on how people look. And I know, uncomfortable as it is for me to admit it, that my every act of walking down the street or through the park is laden with distinctions between me and "the other," and that regrettable as I may find the latest news item rooted in profiling, I do not find it surprising. I know the sense of security I feel when a police car pulls up next to me, and I know that that my experience is not shared by all people of color. I know that, startled and grieved as I am by a world marked by the offenses wrought by bias, I am not shocked. In my own limited sphere, am I not myself guilty of the same?

And I know that when I turn the lens onto the Jewish community, my own community, here, too, I come up wanting. I am given pause when I think of the Jewish mother of color who shared with me her frustration because she was presumed to be a nanny by other parents at drop-off. I am given pause by the experience of a child of color at her Jewish summer camp who was teased by the other kids for not being Jewish. I conduct an audit of my staff, my programs, and my own words, and I know there is still much work to be done. Confessions of bias need not be damning; they are opportunities to acknowledge the work that needs to be done. Leadership means it is not enough to talk the talk; we need to walk the walk. There is work to be done because building an inclusive community is a self-fulfilling prophecy. If I want the next generation of children at Park Avenue Synagogue to believe that a Jew of color is unremarkable, then I must make it unremarkable. If I want my children or, more likely, grandchildren not to inherit or internalize deeply ingrained notions of race, then I myself must work to eliminate the structures that serve to perpetuate those notions. It is not enough to consider yourself one of the good guys and go about your business. You have to check your implicit biases; you have to live intentionally knowing they are present; and then you have to work on the much broader and deeper societal transformations that await.

Our Torah reading describes inequity based on gender, not race, recounting how the disenfranchised daughters of Tzelophehad successfully transformed the biblical laws of inheritance. The medieval commentator Rashi attributes their success to the fact that they saw with their eyes what Moses's eyes did not. The first step is to open our eyes. Only then can we effectuate structural change. It is not easy, but it is not impossible, and the good news is that it is in all of our power to do so.

Until twenty-four hours ago, the parting image of this sermon was going to be the final public appearance of Greenberg and Robinson, brought together to testify before the Supreme Court on behalf of Curt Flood against the reserve clause. A closing scene and fitting tribute to their friendship, which I encourage you to read about.

But then something really unexpected happened in Pittsburgh.

This time, the sport was football. As you may have heard, earlier this week Philadelphia wide receiver DeSean Jackson posted a screed against Jews, as significant for its offensive nature as for the fact that the recently woke NFL has been as silent on Jackson's antisemitism as it has been vocal of late on any racism.

About thirty-six hours ago, Pittsburgh offensive tackle Zach Banner posted a response to Jackson that I encourage you to read or listen to in full. In brief, without platitudes, banalities, or anger, Banner, who is of Chamorro and African American descent, addresses Jackson and his antisemitism, seeking to correct the misbelief among Black and Brown people regarding Jews. Having spoken of his Jewish friends and his horror at the Pittsburgh shooting, Banner preaches that important as the work of Black Lives Matter may be, its achievements can't come by way of stepping on the backs of other people, meaning Jews. In Banner's own words: "We can't preach equality but as a result we're just trying to flip the script and change the hierarchy. . . . Change your heart, put your arm around people, and let's all uplift each other." (*Tablet*, July 8, 2020)

Who would think that some 70 years after that 1947 day in Pittsburgh, it would be an African American athlete in the same city who would call out his own community on prejudice against Jews? Bias operates in every direction, sometimes all at the same time, and the pressures of our moment run the risk of bringing out the worst in people, not the best. Our shared human condition alerts us to the fact that we are all flawed and that we are all capable of doing better. So let's do what Greenberg did in 1947, what Heschel preached in 1963, and what Banner posted this past week. Change our hearts, put our arms around people, and uplift each other. It is not everything, but it is something and it is certainly better than nothing. It is, you might say, first base. But maybe, just maybe, from there we will round the bases together, creating a world able to house the hopes and dreams we all share for our children and grandchildren.

Rosenberg, Yair, "Zach Banner Stands Up for the Jews." *Tablet*, July 8, 2020 https://www.tabletmag.com/sections/news/articles/zach-banner-desean-jackson-anti-semitism

December 8, 2019
10 Kislev 5780

Our Hanukkah:
Rededication of the 87th Street Building

The Talmud asks a question about this month's upcoming festival of lights that is as basic as it is essential: *Mai Hanukkah*, Aramaic for "what is Hanukkah?" Hanukkah, explain the Rabbis, means "rededication," recalling when the Maccabees, having defeated their Greek oppressors, entered the Temple to rededicate it to service to God. Like our ancestors of old, like our congregation's founders who crossed the threshold in the 1880s as we reenacted today, like our intrepid leaders who laid the cornerstone of this building in 1927, like our bold forerunners who established the Steinberg House in 1954, like our courageous predecessors who built the Rita and George Shapiro House in 1980, today, we, the present members of Park Avenue Synagogue, claim our Hanukkah. Our rededication of this sacred space, which together with the Eli M. Black Lifelong Learning Center will serve the hopes and dreams of our community present and future.

Yes, Hanukkah means rededication, but as the Talmud explains, as any of our congregational school students will tell you, the story of Hanukkah is not only about a physical building. It is about a miracle, a miracle that occurred when Judah Maccabee and his brothers entered the Temple in such need of renewal and found a single cruse of oil with the seal of the high priest – not nearly enough for the task at hand. But what they lacked in oil, they more than made up for in

Our Hanukkah: Rededication of the 87th Street Building   183

faith: faith in themselves, faith in their God, and faith in the Jewish future. One day became two, which became three, one day after the next, one light after another, the flame shining brighter and brighter, more and more people pitching in, one after the other after the other, everyone doing their part, each person inspired by their neighbor, doing what they could until that Temple stood worthy of God's presence. And that, explains the Talmud, is what the miracle of Hanukkah was, and that is what the miracle of Hanukkah has been throughout the ages, whenever a Jewish community has worked collectively to secure our people's future. That is the recurring miracle of this community in 1882, in 1927, in 1954, in 1980, and today.

Today's celebration reflects over five years of vision and hard work by dedicated professionals and lay leaders. Today's celebration reflects the cumulative efforts of some 137 years of congregational history. But most of all, today's celebration reflects the efforts of each and every one of you here in this Sanctuary, on the third floor, on livestream, and on the streets. You, the present membership of Park Avenue Synagogue have made today's miracle possible by means of your faith, your love of our people and of this community, and your commitment to our shared future.

As with that first Hanukkah, our story began with a single cruse of oil – adorned with the seal not of the high priest, but of Hess. Truth be told, that cruse of oil was not so small, but its real importance was in being the first. As the rabbis teach: *tov shem tov mi-shemen tov*, a good name is more valuable that fine oil. Just as the 1980 building was only possible thanks to the good name of Leon and Norma Hess of blessed memory, so the good name of John and Susan Hess has inspired so many others to follow their lead. Susan and John, may your home and the home of your children and grandchildren be blessed with all good things, as you have blessed our community. I am so very grateful to you for your constant friendship that spans the generations. And in the presence of Leon and Debra Black, David and Jackie Simon, and Ralph and Ricky Lauren, thank you to each of you and your families, who as co-chairs together with John and Susan have lent your good names and your support to inspire so many others toward this effort to transform the physical footprint of our community. From our campaign chairs to our campaign committee to the membership of this congregation, 97 percent of you. As in the Temple of old, drop by drop, hour by hour, day by day, meeting to meeting, people pitching in their time, talent, and treasure.

Today is here! Let it sink in, breathe in that feeling. Enjoy it. If we are lucky, a day like this happens once in a lifetime, and that moment, friends, is here and now. This is the wonder of what a community can accomplish when they work together towards a shared goal. Enjoy the feeling today and in the years ahead, retrieve it every time you cross the threshold into this building reciting the words of *Mah Tovu*, inscribed on the corner of the building at 87th and Madison.

It may not be the crossing of the sea or the sun standing still, but make no mistake, the Hanukkah miracle of today, made possible by way of the work of your hands, is altogether worthy of God's blessing. But let me tell you the most important thing about today, about the feeling that you have, that I have, that we all have in this hour. Yes, we have created something extraordinary, physical building, but that is just the beginning.

The book of Proverbs teaches that the soul of a person is the light of God. In other words, there is a divine spark within us all – an internal and eternal spark of the divine which, when joined with others, can do remarkable things. Today it is about a building, but tomorrow and the next day and the next day after that, those divine sparks can be made manifest and leveraged towards building the shared spiritual architecture of this community. We can sign up for classes, come to Shabbat services, perform deeds of kindness, light Shabbat candles, go to minyan, visit the sick, feed the hungry, do mitzvot, and commit to the needs of the Jewish people, of Israel and of our shared humanity. We can be the Jews and the Jewish community we aspire to be, and this synagogue can lead the charge for American Jewry. If we can build this building together, just think about what we can accomplish if we continue to pool together the most valuable thing that each one of us has: the divine spark within. The mission of this synagogue is to inspire, educate and support our membership towards living passion-filled Jewish lives, and we are just getting started. Ultimately, friends, the success of our building rededication will be measured not by today's festivities, but by whether our future selves and future generations will prove worthy of the commitments affirmed in this sacred hour.

Mai Hanukkah? What is Hanukkah? Hanukkah means rededication. Rededication of this synagogue as a house of prayer, a house of learning and a house of community – of course. Rededication to the values of *tikkun olam*, memory, peoplehood, worship, Jewish culture, learning, Israel, and community – absolutely. But most of all, Hanukkah is a rededication to the proposition that there is no limit to the wonders that we can achieve when we work together toward realizing a shared vision. Today a building, tomorrow . . . so many dreams to realize. Again and again, and into the years ahead, may we be blessed to cross the threshold of our shared potential together.

Park Avenue Synagogue
138th Annual Meeting

Unfortunate as our present circumstance may be, prompting our annual congregational meeting to be rescheduled to this date on a virtual platform, it does provide us the opportunity to fulfil a mitzvah together as a community: counting the final night of the Omer, the forty-nine days between the spring festival of Passover and tomorrow night's festival of Shavuot.

Hineni mukḥan um'zuman l'kayem mitzvat aseh shel s'firat ha-omer, k'mo shekatuv ba-torah: U-s'fartem lakhem mi-moḥarat ha-shabbat, miyom havi·akhem et omer hat'nufah, sheva shabbatot t'mimot tihiyenah, ad mi-moḥarat ha-shabbat ha-sh'vi·it tisp'ru ḥamishim yom.

Behold, I am ready and prepared to fulfill the mitzvah of counting the Omer, as it says in the Torah: "You shall count from the eve of the second day of Pesach, when an omer of grain is to be brought as an offering, seven complete weeks. The day after the seventh week of your counting will make fifty days." (Leviticus 23:15–16)

Barukh atah Adonai eloheinu melekh ha-olam, asher kidshanu b'mitzvotav v'tzivanu al s'firat ha-omer.

Hayom tisha v'arbaim yom, she-hem shivah shavuot la-omer.
Today is forty-nine days, which are seven weeks of the Omer.

I will readily admit that before this year, the counting of the Omer has never been an easy mitzvah for me to fulfill. It is hardly high on the list of core observances of our people, and even those of us who are diligent enough to remember to begin counting on the second night of Passover rarely have the presence of mind to continue every evening for the next forty-eight days. Doing a mitzvah that requires continual attention over an extended period of time is only made more difficult by the obscurity of the custom's origins. In the Torah, it is explained as an expression of the farmer's gratitude for his bounty – an "omer" being a measurement of barley brought to the Temple each day. Following the destruction of the Temple, the Omer came to represent the counting of the days themselves. In the Talmud, this period is marked by mourning in remembrance of a time of catastrophic loss for the students of Rabbi Akiva. By the time of Maimonides, the Omer had become the ritualized link between the Exodus from Egypt and the giving of the Torah at Mount Sinai. In Kabbalistic literature, each week and each day came to be associated with God's mystical attributes. There are a lot of really good interpretations of the mitzvah of counting of the Omer – and no really great ones – which is probably why I come up with gimmicks like listing the professional athletes whose jersey numbers correspond to each day. Is it surprising that so many good Jews, myself included, have trouble fulfilling this seasonal mitzvah day after day after day?

And yet, this year I did exactly that. Every evening, when my wife and children were finished with their Zoom commitments, when I was done with my Zoom meetings and classes, when we sat down for dinner in a manner that we simply would not do in normal circumstances, we began the meal with the Omer brakhah. There have been times over the years that I have exaggerated aspects of my family life – that I sing Sh'ma to each kid every night as I tuck them in, that I drop them off at school every day. Sometimes a preacher has to take a little homiletic license to drive home a point. But on this one, on counting the Omer, you have my word that every night without fail, it was a flawless run, to be completed with my family later this evening: a track record notable not just for its perfection but also – and it is this point I want to focus on – for the ease of its fulfillment.

Why was I able to fulfill this otherwise elusive mitzvah this year? It was not, I know, because I felt more convinced of its origins: the Omer remains as mysterious and enigmatic as ever. What I am convinced of, both at each evening's counting and now, in reflection, is that this mitzvah brought a degree of predictability and structure into a period of time that, like the fourth book of the bible in which we find ourselves, can best be understood as a midbar, a wilderness. Our lives have been put on hold; the future is not at all clear, one day leading to the next to the next to the next. Yes, we are having end-of-year congregational meetings; some are celebrating graduations; many have suffered loss; and some have welcomed new life. But be it because so many of us are sheltering in place or because we find ourselves on the proverbial tarmac waiting interminably for take-off, we find ourselves without question thirsting for a spiritual scaffold in ways we otherwise would not. We are in want of relationships and rhythms that would normally shape our lives and we have discovered that there is meaning in rituals, mitzvot like counting the omer, that might not otherwise be quite so reachable.

I am reminded of Daniel Defoe's famous novel The Life and Adventures of Robinson Crusoe, where the first decisive act Robinson Crusoe performs after being cast ashore on a desert island is to contrive a calendar and begin to count the days and weeks. He writes:

> "After I had been there about ten or twelve days, it came into my thought that I should lose my reckoning of time for want of book, and pen and ink, and should even forget the Sabbath days."

To prevent this, Crusoe tells us, he set up a great post on the shore. After inscribing on it with his knife the date of his arrival on the island, he proceeded to mark the days and Sabbaths and months and years as they passed:

> "I cut every day a notch with my knife, and every seventh notch was as long again as the rest, and every first day of the month as long again as that long one; and thus I kept my calendar, or weekly, monthly, and yearly reckoning of time."

For our shipwrecked friend, but really for all of us, this counting, this spiritual scaffold, became an essential act of humanity, providing structure to our wilderness experience.

Long before COVID-19, I had been well convinced of the importance of any synagogue. and specifically our synagogue, in the lives of its members. The Torah that is taught, the prayers that are offered, the community that is formed, and the lifecycle events – whether of celebration or of sorrow – made sacred by way of our covenanted community. Truth be told, when we vacated the building, I was not sure what the next day would bring. Was it not, after all, just this past December that we dedicated our magnificent new space? Would Torah still be taught, would prayers still be offered, would community survive without being able to enter our temple at 87th and Madison?

And while I would readily forgo any acquired wisdom if doing so would provide relief from our present pain and loss, this evening, some forty-nine days and change since we received our shelter-in-place orders, I can share that I have never been as convinced, as affirmed, and as confident in the project of Park Avenue Synagogue as I am today. Like counting the Omer, I have seen that for the members of our community, the goods and services (literal and spiritual) we provide have become more important, not less. There is more, not less, thirst for learning, for Jewish engagement, for spiritual and intellectual uplift, and for the bonds of community: A post-minyan class, normally attended by a modest sixteen or so participants, now at sixty and growing; Shabbat services, always well attended, now overflowing with online viewers; a Zoom bris with screen after screen of attendees offering the joy of community; the burgeoning demand by our youngest learners for PAS celebrity music educator Josh Rosenberg. And in loss, painful loss, even here I am affirmed of the role the synagogue plays to help our members navigate through unspeakable grief – the compassion of my clergy colleagues at a distance, but ever-present, in hospital rooms, at gravesides, and in shiva houses.

It is not merely a matter of increased engagement or that people have time on their hands. In this time of uncertainty, in this wilderness, our synagogue, our faith, our rituals have become more, not less important. The other day I spoke with a proudly secular member of the community, a man who "married into this Jewish thing." Ritual does not come naturally to him. "Rabbi," he said, "Shabbat has never meant as much to me as it does now." A young man, a new father, his child born under quarantine, called me the other day asking me how to bless his child. Despite all the uncertainty, or maybe precisely because of it, he wanted to bless his child according to tradition. If you have watched our Bnei Mitzvah on any given shabbat, if you pause to unpack what is taking place, what is really taking place, then you will appreciate the raw, authentic, and pure expression of ritual – without the party, without the presents. It is not just quantity; this wilderness has resulted in a thirst for a quality of engagement with our tradition. Again, I would give it all up in a heartbeat, but if you want a case statement for Park Avenue Synagogue, if you wanted to plead the case for the thirsting soul of American Jewry, then you need look no further than these past weeks.

And all of this comes by virtue of our being blessed by having the best synagogue staff ever fielded. The clergy team, the education team, the administration team, the maintenance team – every team member from the security guard opening the building in the morning to the Bnei Mitzvah tutor trying her darndest to teach your kid to sing on key. From the Early Childhood Educator reinventing how education happens in a virtual world to the accounting professional figuring how to send statements in a paperless world. From the tech engineer making sure our services are streaming to the communications team making sure you can register for your next class online. Even our rabbinic intern Viki Bedo was just named by The Jewish Week as one of this year's top "36 under 36." To work at Park Avenue means to work collaboratively, creatively, and with a self-demand for excellence – always extending the potential for synagogue life and striving to make potentialities into realities.

And how is it all made possible? By invested and committed lay leadership: our arms and committees, our advisory council, our board, and our officers under the leadership of Chairman Marc Becker and President Natalie Barth. There are always moving pieces, concerns both short-term and long-term, strategies and tactics to be considered, funds to be raised, budgets to be made and lay leaders to be inspired. Every lay leader is a volunteer with no shortage of personal and professional commitments outside of the synagogue. And yet they show up every day, stewards of our synagogue, servants to our membership, always guided by what is best for the community. I would be remiss if I did not share how grateful I am for the abiding confidence and counsel the lay leadership extends to me personally and to the entire staff. Indeed, when a future volume of congregational history is written, and someone retrieves the dusty words spoken this evening in order to write the chapter that will describe how we fared during this difficult time, a chapter that will be followed by countless other chapters, let it be noted that it was the trust shared between lay and professional leadership that was our north star as we navigated these uncharted waters.

The paradox of our synagogue moment is that we are, at one and the same time, living in the worst of times and in the best of times. There is pain, there is loss, and there is uncertainty. And . . . never before has our synagogue played as vital, stabilizing, and essential role as it is playing today. So let us grab hold of the polarities of the hour – this paradox thrust upon us – and let us lean in. The moment calls for sacrifice, for leadership, for philanthropic audacity, and for faith. Let us respond in spirit and deed with a nobility of purpose that bespeaks our people's highest ideals.

No different than the Israelites of old, tonight we stand at the base of a mountain unsure of what tomorrow will bring. One step at a time, together, we will climb. We will continue on our journey and we will, assuredly, reach the promised land.

Louis Jacobs:
A Man for Our Time

On the 100th anniversary of his birth, finding new meaning in the work of the great British theologian

Judaism has a way of finding meaning in its darkest hours, turning catastrophes into opportunities for contemplation, change, and growth. Just as the emergence of rabbinic Judaism occurred in the wake of the destruction of Jerusalem's Temple and the flowering of Jewish mysticism followed the expulsion of Spanish Jewry, the efflorescence of Jewish theological discourse in the 1950s and 1960s can be traced to the ruptures wrought by the social upheavals of the preceding decades. "Philosophy," Abraham Joshua Heschel summed up this point neatly, "cannot be the same after Auschwitz and Hiroshima."

Case in point is Heschel's British contemporary, Rabbi Dr. Louis Jacobs, who passed away in 2006 and whose 100th birthday would be celebrated this week. Jacobs may be less known to American Jews, but his presence continues to loom large in the Anglo-Jewish consciousness, and his work is one we should re-read, especially now that the world is again facing a transformative crisis.

Jacobs is most remembered for his exclusion in the early 1960s from prominent rabbinical seminary post and pulpit. Often explained as a drama in two acts, the "Jacobs Affair" began when then Chief Rabbi Israel Brodie refused to promote Jacobs to the principalship of Anglo-Jewish Orthodoxy's ministerial training institution, Jews College, resulting in Jacobs and like-minded lay leaders to resign in protest. The second act played out two years later, when Brodie refused to certify Jacobs as theologically fit to return to his New West End pulpit, resulting in the resignation of hundreds of members and the eventual establishment of the independent New London Synagogue, a congregation that Jacobs would lead with distinction into the decades to come. The controversy surrounding Jacobs's persona spilled onto the pages of the Jewish and non-Jewish press, a *kulturkampf* that continues to be referenced as a major pivot in British Jewry's self-understanding.

While the ostensible bone of contention between Jacobs and his opponents revolved around Jacobs's 1957 book *We Have Reason to Believe*, which pondered the question of whether the Torah is or isn't from heaven, with hindsight we know that far more than matters of scriptural authority were at stake. The debates surrounding revelation reflected a shell-shocked Jewish community's grappling with their post-Holocaust condition. Put differently, asking whether God did or did not write the Torah can be understood as another way of asking a much more immediate, thorny, and painful question, namely where was God in Auschwitz. The agitated theological spirit that guided Jacobs was not limited to the Jewish community: Be it Billy Graham's evangelical revivalist crusades or the "Honest to God" debates of the Church of England, the 1950s and 1960s challenged and divided the full spectrum of religious life.

But it's not so much for his contributions to theology that we must remember Jacobs today; instead, he leaves us with a shining example of unflinching courage in responding to the challenges of the day, an abiding intellectual honesty, and a steadfast belief that the spiritual vocabulary to meet those challenges can be found within traditional Jewish sources.

All of which begs the question: In the face of a pandemic, what would Louis Jacobs say? It is not Auschwitz or Hiroshima, but we are living through a trauma and transformation the likes of which we have never experienced. In addition to questions of human loss and suffering, COVID has touched on every aspect of our existence—economic, educational, communal, political, interpersonal and otherwise. The foundations of our very being are being tested and reconsidered. How do we form community given limitations on public assembly? How shall we build and sustain relationships in a time of quarantine? How can we draft life plans in the face of an unknown future?

COVID has brought the fault lines of our society into full relief.

What exactly are our obligations to the other and towards forming a more just society? In a rapidly changing landscape marked by a paucity of information and reliable leadership, to whom shall we turn to for authority, ethics, morality and truth? As humanity stays in place in response to the spread of an unseen and deadly virus, what exactly do conventional borders and boundaries mean, between nations and people alike? How shall our rituals, houses of worship and communal structures respond to the challenges of the hour? Are our religious identities essential to our being, or discretionary claims that can be waived in times of crisis?

We do not yet have the luxury of looking back in retrospect, hence it is premature to ask how future theology will respond to the present hour. Yet even from the eye of the storm we see the questions emerge on suffering, community, self, and God. As a colleague recently reflected to me: How can over seven billion people experience a brush with death and not emerge asking new philosophical and theological questions?

Had Louis Jacobs lived to witness our present crisis, I would like to imagine he would draw from his encyclopedic knowledge of Jewish law to demonstrate how Jewish practice must transform to meet the needs of the moment. I would like to think that his studies of Jewish ethical literature would provide guidance for a humanity in desperate need of a moral compass. Perhaps his studies of Jewish mysticism could provide the spiritual vocabulary of personal and communal sacrifice that would help ease the daily travails afflicting so many. Jacobs's studies on the relationship between particularism and universalism, between the individual and the community would offer much needed guidance on clarifying the Jewish obligation to the other and the urgent imperative to establish a just society. As a theologian of first rank, no doubt Jacobs would want to guide a searching humanity as to how to affirm faith in God in the face of suffering—helping us find reason to believe. As a rabbi ministering his flock, I believe that Jacobs would believe his primary responsibility to be demonstrating how, even and perhaps especially in times of crisis, the canon of Jewish literature can respond with relevance to the exigencies of a pandemic.

Let this, then, be this great man's legacy, the constant seeking of synthesis between the permanent values and truth of tradition and the best thought of the day. If we find a way to bind together a deep love for the Jewish people and a profound respect for our shared humanity, we will be able to, like Louis Jacobs, weather even the most daunting of crises.

Reprinted with permission from Tablet, July 17, 2020
   https://www.tabletmag.com/sections/belief/articles/louis-jacobs-man-for-our-time

Rabbi Cosgrove's dissertation, "Teyku: The Insoluble Contradictions in the Life and Thought of Louis Jacobs," was completed in 2008.

Park Avenue Synagogue

Park Avenue Synagogue – *Agudat Yesharim*, The Association of the Righteous – is one of the leading congregations of the Conservative movement. The synagogue's "family tree" includes several congregations that merged over multiple decades. The earliest of them, Gates of Hope, was founded in 1882. Some twelve years after its founding, the synagogue joined with Congregation Agudat Yesharim, which became the Hebrew name of the merged congregation.

In 1923, the congregation was known as Eighty-Sixth Street Temple/Agudat Yesharim, after further integrating with the Seventy-Second Street Temple (itself a product of the earlier merger of two congregations that had their beginnings on the Lower East Side in the 1840s, Beth Israel and Bikkur Cholim). A last merger took place in 1928 with the addition of Atereth Israel, a congregation of Alsatian Jews who worshipped in their building on East 82nd Street before the congregation petitioned the State of New York to change its name to Park Avenue Synagogue. In March of 1927, the renamed congregation dedicated the building on 87th Street, which is our sanctuary today. It is one of the last synagogues built in the Moorish style, which first became popular in Europe in the 1850s.

When Rabbi Milton Steinberg came to the pulpit in 1933, Park Avenue Synagogue joined the Conservative movement. In 1954, the Milton Steinberg House was built adjacent to the sanctuary building and dedicated to the memory of the late rabbi. The building's façade was a unique stained-glass window wall created by the abstract expressionist artist Adolph Gottlieb (1903-1974). The windows include 21 compositions representing traditional Jewish emblems, religious rituals, biblical incidents, and holidays.

During the next quarter-century, with the burgeoning of the Upper East Side into a major Jewish community, the congregation outgrew its building. The dream for more space was coupled with the idea of making a new building a living memorial to the more than one million Jewish children who perished during the Holocaust. In 1980, the Steinberg building was incorporated into the Rita and George M. Shapiro House. With two bronze sculptures by Nathan Rapoport on its façade, this building expressed the hope that Park Avenue Synagogue would inspire new generations of educated and proud Jews and ensure the continuity of Jewish tradition, history, faith, and heritage.

In 2014, with more and more of its 1,700 member families actively engaging in synagogue life, Park Avenue Synagogue was once again bursting at the seams. The community undertook a once-in-a-generation project to expand by adding the Eli M. Black Lifelong Learning Center at 11 East 89th Street, dedicated in October 2017, and by reimagining the interior of the 87th Street building, rededicated in December 2019. The historic Gottlieb windows have been repurposed in both buildings to link the Lifelong Learning Center with the revitalized 87th Street building. With Jewish texts and images integrated into the very walls of both buildings, the new campus serves Park Avenue Synagogue's mission to create more and better pathways for learning, engagement, and inclusion in order to enhance the Jewish experience for all of members of the community.

Park Avenue Synagogue
Board of Trustees, Clergy, and Staff, 2020-2021

Officers
Marc Becker, *Chairman*
Natalie W. Barth, *President*
Lizzy Markus, *Vice President*
Nan Rubin, *Vice President*
Amy Steiner, *Vice President*
Mark First, *Treasurer*
Craig Solomon, *Associate Treasurer*
Mark Hirsch, *Secretary*

Honorary Chairmen
Amy A.B. Bressman
Joel J. Cohen
Geoffrey J. Colvin
Steven M. Friedman
Alan Levine
Martin J. Milston
Arthur Penn

Honorary Presidents
Robert P. Antler
Paul M. Corwin
Brian G. Lustbader
Menachem Z. Rosensaft
Paul S. Schreiber

Honorary Officers
Barry A. Bryer
Marcia Eppler Colvin
Joanne V. Davis
Rachael S. First
Eleanor Frommer
Bernard Goldberg
Martin Halbfinger
Joel Hirschtritt
Marlene Muskin
David Parker
Jean Bloch Rosensaft
Howard Rubin
Melvin L. Schweitzer
Susan Brous Silverman
Heidi Silverstone
Adam Usdan

Clergy and Staff
Elliot J. Cosgrove, PhD, *Rabbi*
Neil Zuckerman, *Rabbi*
Ethan H. Witkovsky, *Rabbi*
Azi Schwartz, *Cantor*
Rachel Brook, *Cantor*
David H. Lincoln, *Rabbi Emeritus*
David Lefkowitz, *Cantor Emeritus*
Beryl P. Chernov, *Executive Director*
Liz Offenbach, *Associate Executive Director*
Rabbi Charles Savenor, *Director of Congregational Education*
Marga Hirsch, *Editor*

Honorary Trustees
Leslie Agisim
Lucy Becker
Jena Berlinski
Daniel Bernstein
Nadine Habousha Cohen
Darcy Dalton
James Druckman
Susan Edelstein
Herb Feiwel
Henry Glanternik
Freema Gluck
Harrison Goldin
Richard S. Green
Katherina Grunfeld
Lynn Halbfinger
Laurie Harris
Ellen Harrow
Nancy I. Hirschtritt
Amos Kaminski
Floy Kaminski
Dennis Karr
Stephanie Leichter
Morris M. Podolsky
Frank Pollak
Judith Poss
Alain Roizen
Willa Rosenberg
Jimmy Rosenfeld
Joann Abrams Rosoff
Suzette Rubinstein
Shereen Gertel Rutman
Joan Schefler
Joan Schreiber
Wendy Slavin
Karen Smul
Marcia Stone
Ray Treiger
Mark Wasserberger
Barbara Weinstein

Trustees
Suzanne Aisenberg
Susan Cantor
Lisa Cohen
Brian Eizenstat
Eric Feuerstein
Edward Fisher
Erica Friedman
Paula Gendel
Lisa Grinberg
Andrew Heller
Jennifer Hoine
Fred Kastenbaum
Dena Klein
Lauren Klein
Andrea Baumann Lustig
Richard Nackenson
Melissa Raskin
Wendy Sacks
Marc Silberberg
Suzi Stadler
Tamara Stark
Vicki Warner
Steven Wasserman
Thom Waye
Meryl Wiener
Jacqui Weidman
Linda Yarden
Pauline Zablow

Advisory Council
Jamie Bahar
Rachel Bluth
David Chasen
Linda Daitz
Steven Darling
Barry Frankel
Gail Furman
Judy Greenblatt
Diane Hess
Devon Klein
Nancy Korff
Stephanie Levey
David Phillips
Stefanie Katz Rothman
Lauren Ruderfer
Stacie Schapiro
Brian Schreiber
Lori Schreiber
Jeffrey Silverman
Rob Silverstone
Susanna Sirefman
Susan Smirnoff
Jordan Solomon
Samantha Tanenbaum
Marissa Zackowitz
Larry Zakarin